Trekking Through Trials

Jacob I. Volkov

Dedication

I dedicate this book to our children: Milla, Michael & Paul (twins), and Alexandra; and to my many nephews and nieces, who "pestered" me to put the Volkov legacies into writing, since I am the last surviving person of my generation, and the only one with a college education. I complied with your request. Here it is. Don't complain.

Gratitude

I wish to extend my gratitude to the following relatives who supplied me with information about the Volkov past.

The first three individuals are no longer alive.

Maria Sevastyanovna Volkova (feminine form of surname Volkov) Kosareva (maiden name), my mother, whose information I trusted the most.

Aunt Anna Danilovna Loskutova (Deryabina) was a good storyteller with a good memory. Her first husband was my youngest uncle, Fyodor Stepanovich Volkov, a dashing man who served in the Soviet cavalry. He died in Persia at the age of thirty-three.

Faina Vasilyevna Jamrashvili, my first cousin, supplied me with information on Prokhladnoye after our escape. This information was otherwise unattainable, as she was left behind and saw the aftermath.

Oleg Nikolayevich Osadtchi, my nephew, provided me with statistical information. He constructed a family tree of the Volkov and Kosarev families.

Evdokia (Dusya) Ivanovna Guseva (Muravyova) provided me with recent information on my subject.

Michael Volkov, our son, helped me with the mysteries of computers. He also produced the map of our trek.

My gratitude also extends to our daughter, Lyudmila (Volkov) Smith, and her son, Edward Trent Smith. They helped make my English writing sound more American.

Most of all, I thank my wife, Zenaida (Zena) Afanasyevna (Maltseva), who put up with me during my labor over this book. My heartfelt gratitude goes to my grandnephew, Mark Kashirsky, for designing the cover for this book. Thanks, Markusha!

My biggest gratitude goes to Svetlana (Lana) Osadtchi, who dedicated an enormous number of weeks to edit this otherwise un-printable book and added additional biblical references. She verified every historic and geographic aspect. No amount of thank-you's could make up for your effort, Lanachka! *Bolshoi spasibo!*

Contents

Part XI

Introduction

Every family has its own unique history that could make for an interesting tale. I use my Volkov family merely as a vehicle through which I wish to present the events and places of the times past, and the experiences that the Volkovs had lived through.

I want you, my descendants, to know that you are a product of godly ancestors who survived through happy and horrible times. During their trekking through trials, they turned to their God for guidance and wisdom, and He rewarded them with miraculous deliverance from oppressions and persecutions.

Please note, I used the International Phonetic Alphabet (IPA) to transliterate non-English words. Also, on March 21, 1935, Persia was renamed Iran. However, I'll be referring to Iran as Persia in the beginning, because "Iran," at this time, did not exist in the refugees' vocabulary.

Part I

Chapter I

The Volkov Roots

For whatever was written in earlier times was written for our instruction, that through perseverance and the encouragement of the Scriptures we might have hope.
Romans 15:4, NASB

Looking back may make you either proud or ashamed of your past, or both. It is good to look back to see where you have been, and what you can learn from your past, avoiding the mistakes that beset you. It is with these thoughts that I write to you of the Volkov past.

The name "Volkov" means "of the wolf." In case you didn't already know, Volkov is a popular name in Russia. You meet people by that name in the royal courts of Ivan IV (Ivan the Terrible) and Catherine II (Catherine the Great); as well as those who are aristocrats, cosmonauts and peasants.

There is one named Fyodor Grigorievich Volkov—Фёдор (Fyodor or Fred, also Theodor) Григориевич (Grigorievich, son of Gregory, a patronymic) Волков (Volkov)—founder of the Russian theater. (Wikipedia)

He and his two brothers would write plays. They acted them out in their father's barn just for the fun of it. People enjoyed the show. Now, it's history. To this day, there is an active theater in Yaroslavl, Russia, named after Fyodor Volkov.

According to my nephew Oleg's research, my great-great grandfather's name was Fadey (Фадей) Volkov. Where he lived is not known. He had a son named, Aleksander.

These ancestors were serfs; in other words, slaves. Like slaves everywhere, they were sold, bought, bartered for, or gifted to someone. People with free spirits make poor slaves.

Like many other young men, Aleksander ran away from his master and ended up somewhere in Central Russia, within the Vladimir and Suzdal regions. This part of Russia is now called the Golden Ring, an area designated as the heart of historic Russia. People having lived in this geographical location are called the Great Russians.

Apparently, Aleksander was a capable businessman. When he died, he left his estate to his first son, Vasiliy Aleksandrovich Volkov

(1844–1920). Vasiliy is remembered as a hospitable person. Aleksander had another son, Stepan Aleksandrovich Volkov (1847–1935), my grandfather. He died in Persia.

These are our distant roots.

Chapter 2

Discovering New Faith

For centuries, reading the Bible or possessing one was considered a crime in Russia. Only the clergy and a few privileged non-clergy had access to the Holy Scriptures. Leaders of the state religion, Orthodoxy, feared that once people started reading the Bible, they might abandon Orthodoxy—hence the tight control.

During the latter part of the 19th century (1800s), Russia began to tolerate the reading of the Bible, slowly at first. Consequently, the authorities' fears had been realized—the serious seekers of the biblical truths began to study the Bible diligently.

This search led to the discovery that many church traditions were not biblical. For example, the veneration of the saints, especially Mary, mother of Jesus, baptism by sprinkling, infant baptism, worshiping of idols or icons (a direct violation of the Second Commandment), just to name a few, are not supported by the Bible.

When your ancestors began to read the Bible, and discovered the discrepancy between church traditions and the Holy Scriptures, they abandoned the non-Biblical traditions; most of them.

Some began observing the biblical seventh-day Sabbath—Saturday. Among such people were our great grandparents on both sides. Some, however, continued honoring the sun day (Sunday). When your great-great grandparents refused to light candles to the saints, bring their infants for baptism, and confess their sins to a priest, there were reprisals from the Church.

This discovery of non-Biblical doctrines became epidemic and many people began to abandon the state religion. This did not sit well with religious leaders who had to find some remedy for this contagion. This was a time in Czarist Russia, before Communism entered the scene.

Decision to leave the state religion launched a turbulent life for many future generations, the rebellious "refuzniks" I have come to name them. For example, when my great-grandparents on my mother's side, the Kosarevs, refused to take their newborn child to church for baptism and stopped attending church altogether, they were incarcerated, in separate cells, for five years.

Officials resorted to deception. They told the wife that her husband had recanted of his "heresy" and agreed to go back to the Mother Church. Then, they told the same ruse to her husband. The couple requested permission to speak with one other. Officials granted their request with stipulation— they were to talk only in the officials' presence.

The prisoners outsmarted the officials and spoke to each other in the Mardvin language. Of course, the ploy became evident. As a result, they were sent back to their respective cells for an additional two years. Altogether, they spent a total of seven years in prison.

Chapter 3

The Exile

When Orthodox leaders realized that "re-fuzniks" were disseminating contagious "heresy," and that their followers were increasing, they sought help from the State. The latter responded, and the solution was found—exile. Many citizens were rounded up, including the Volkovs and the Kosarevs. They were expelled to the Turkish border, an area called Kars.

Throughout history, this territory had passed from one nation to another. At one time it was part of Persia, then Armenia, then Georgia, then Turkey, then Russia, then back to Turkey. Presently, this area is in Turkish possession. It went back and forth like a ball on a tennis court. At the time of this particular exile, Kars belonged to Russia.

To strengthen its borders, Russia used to banish recalcitrants with their families to sensitive regions of the empire. That is the reason for my relatives' exile to Kars. These "rebels" had to adapt to a different environment, but they praised God for this expulsion.

For once, no one interfered with their beliefs, and being the hardworking people that they were, they soon prospered under peaceful conditions. In the end, their punishment had turned into a blessing.

Part II

Chapter 4

Sevastyan Semyonovich Kosarev

During long wintery nights while in the process of needlework, my mother, Maria Sevastyanovna Volkova, used to tell us interesting stories about her father, Sevastyan Semyonovich Kosarev. She said that he was a devout religious person, a true seeker of Biblical truths, and that he had been given some visions from God.

In Russia at that time, young people were drafted into military service by lottery. The duration of the service was twenty years. To them the military service might as well have been a life sentence—a funeral of sorts. One day, the Kosarev family received a summons for my uncle, Yakov Sevastyanovich Kosarev, directing him to report to the induction center on a certain date. On the eve of the appointed day, Sevastyan, my maternal grandfather, gathered all of his family to pray for Yakov.

The family formed a circle and asked Yakov to kneel in the middle of it, and father (the family patriarch) began to pray. As he prayed, he was shown a vision, in which he saw Yakov covered with a cloak. Then he saw an angel with a long-handled hook. Using the hook, the heavenly Being picked the cloak off Yakov and placed it aside. The vision ended. Sevastyan Semyonovich then turned to all present and announced with assurance that Yakov will not be drafted into the military service.

Early the following morning, grandfather Sevastyan woke up the family to bless Yakov again. According to custom, all members of the family washed, combed their hair, and dressed properly before approaching God. As on the previous evening, they blessed Yakov. Then, each member of the family, in order of age, approached Yakov and gave him a hearty hug and a kiss on the mouth. Even though they were given heavenly assurance that Yakov would not be drafted, there was some shedding of tears.

When father and son appeared at the induction center, the place was crowded. Mothers were crying on their young sons' shoulders. Fathers supported their wives and their sons. Loud weeping and wailing filled the spacious hall. The scene was funereal. It was a veritable funeral, except that it forestalled the death. No one tried to quell the cacophony, as if it were a necessary part of life.

Suddenly a loud voice summoned Yakov Kosarev to approach the lottery box. With trepidation, Yakov reached into the box, pulled out a ticket, and handed it to the attendant. The latter took the ticket, looked at it, and announced, "Number 37," meaning "subject for draft." The confidence on Yakov's face instantly evaporated. His father leaned to his son and whispered, "Don't worry, son. You will be released." With mixed emotions, father and son headed home.

They didn't have to wait long before they received another summons. This time Yakov was to appear before the health commission on November 26, 1897. With apprehension, Yakov appeared before the medical council. At the end of the examination, he was released for further instructions.

Soon he received another letter stating that he was unfit for military duty, indefinitely. With the certificate of release from military duty was included a list of reasons as follows:

CERTIFICATE

SUMMONS BEFORE THE MILITARY DRAFT

(INDEFINITE)

The *resident of the Village Prokhladnoye of Kars County and Region, Kosarev, Yakov Sevastyanovich,* appeared before the military draft in the year of *1897* and, according to the lottery, number *thirty-seven,* was subject for draft to active military duty; however, according to the certificate of physical examination, he is declared unfit for military duty. Consequently, he is released from service forever.

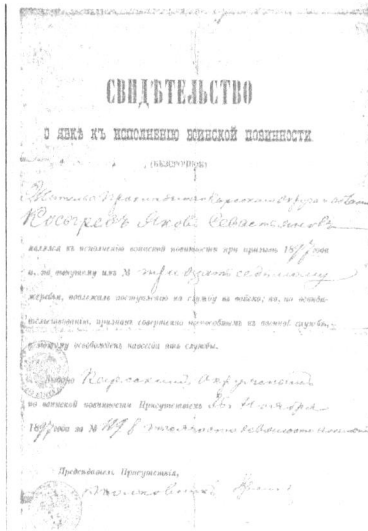

Place of issue: *Kars County,* Dated: *26 November, 1897, #1198 one thousand one hundred ninety-eight.*
Attendant Chairman, *Captain's signature.*

"Here are the reasons for release from military duty:

1) Each person participating in the lottery but due to health issues, having been declared totally unfit for military service, is issued a certificate stating that this person is released from conscription and military duty indefinitely.

2) Such certificates of release concerning the draft for military duty are issued to persons who have passed the age of draft, recently married, and who have entered government or social work."

✳   ✳   ✳

My mom told me of other visions her father had been shown. Here is another incident that comes to mind. Being an avid seeker of truth, Sevastyan, with fasting and praying, launched a quest for additional Biblical truths.

After serious study of the Scriptures, he came across something he had not expected: the sanctity of Sabbath as the true day of worship. Saturday, in Russian, is called *Subbota* and translates to *Sabbath.*

He went back to the Bible. This time he concentrated his research on Biblical authority and command to honor Sunday as the holy day of worship. He pleaded with God to help him find the answer to his perplexity.

In a few days, a vision appeared. In this revelation, the Angel confirmed Sevastyan's discovery regarding the sacredness of Subbota, the seventh day, as being holy to God.

From that day on, he resolved to honor the true day of worship—Saturday.

He could not convince his family to follow him, so he bribed his daughter, my mother, Maria Sevastyanovna. He told her, "If you'll keep the Sabbath holy, I'll buy you a sarafan," something like a jumper. My mother decided that for a sarafan she would keep the Sabbath. From that day on, she never went back to Sunday. Later, she married my father, Isay Stepanovich Volkov, also a Sabbath-keeper.

Maria Sevastyanovna Kosarev (author's mother), with a brother.

From left: (Author's parents) Maria Sevastyanovna and (behind) Isay Stepanovich Volkov, with their firstborn, Aleksey; 2ⁿᵈ in seated row is (Grandfather) Sevastyan Semyonovich Kosarev with family.

Chapter 5

More Trials into Blessings

The onset of the 20th century brought restlessness to the Kars population. The Russo-Japanese War of 1904, World War I (WWI), the Russian Revolution, the turbulence in Turkey across the border, and the subscription of young men into the military—all of these events boded bad times. The residents of Kars County had to seek a safer place for survival. The Kosarevs spent sleepless nights discussing their situation. In prayer and fasting, they presented their case before God and asked for wisdom and guidance. They were impressed to migrate to America.

The final day of farewell arrived. With weeping and sighing, kissing and hugging, for the last time, the Kosarevs loaded their possessions. They headed to the unknown, trusting in God's guidance.

The Volkovs, on the other hand, remained behind. Some of the Volkov men were in the military service, and Stepan Aleksandrovich Volkov, the patriarch of the clan, did not want to break up his sons' family.

* * *

During WWI, the Ottoman Turks took possession of Kars on March 3, 1918 (WP). My mother said, "One evening, we went to bed in Russia, and woke up in Turkey."

The Turkish government was gracious to the Russian settlers in that region. They offered them three options: 1) Remain where they were and live as before, and accept Turkish citizenship. That sounded good. No religious repression from Russian government. On the other hand, there was a catch to it. Their sons were to be drafted into military service, and besides, there was too much unknown; 2) Pack up all their possessions, including all the cattle, and return back to Russia; 3) If those options were not to their liking, they could leave Turkey and go to any country of their choosing. Once again, in prayer, fasting, and supplication, several families including the Volkovs decided to take the second of the three options—return to Russia, whence they were exiled.

Chapter 6

Starting All Over Again

Suddenly, the citizens of Russia became refugees of what was once their own country. They appealed to the Russian authorities for permission to resettle in their previous roots, within the Golden Ring, from which they were exiled. When the authorities discovered the reason for their exile, they turned to the Church. The Church denied the request.

The saying, "Man proposes, but God disposes," became true in the lives of these godly people. Man, with his shortsightedness, never has an inkling of what God has in store for him. In this situation, God had provided a better place for them—even before the problem had arisen.

The refugees were directed to settle in Turkmenistan, another sensitive area of the Russian empire, the border between Russia and Persia.

✳   ✳   ✳

Turkmenistan, formerly Turkmenia, has a long history. This territory on the Silk Road was at one time part of the Persian Empire, until it was ceded to the Russians in 1881 (WP). In the same year, the Russians established a military fortress on a hill to secure the territory for their empire. They named this fortress Poltoratsk (1919 - 1927), after a highly decorated general, Vladimir Alekseyevich Poltoratsky (1828-1889) (WP).

It was necessary to establish such a garrison in that area, because in the forested mountains lived marauding tribes of Tatars that frequently raided the Russian population—plundering cattle, horses, and even humans. Later, this fort was renamed Ashgabat, meaning "Abode of Love" in Farsi. It is presently the capital of Turkmenistan.

On May 13, 1925, Turkmenistan became part of the Soviet Union as the Turkmen Soviet Socialist Republic (Turkmen SSR or Soviet Turkmenia). (WP) Along the southeastern edge of the Caspian Sea, Turkmenistan borders Iran. Although the largest territory of this country is desert, this particular region is ideal for farming and animal husbandry.

✻   ✻   ✻

Back to the Volkovs. To compensate these "immigrants" for refusing to resettle them in their previous homeland, the Czarist government offered them homestead. This included a fifteen-year reprieve from taxation and military service. Because of this agreement, all men in military service were discharged to join their families, including the Volkov men. It was a bittersweet bait, or a pacifier, if you please—good land, dangerous environment.

They formed a village and called it Prokhladnoye (Прохладное), meaning "the cool place." Some families opted to settle in another close-by place called Selyukli (Селюкли).

These families realized that what they thought was a disappointment, was the very place where God wanted them to settle. They had already experienced God's care over them in Kars. Once again, they resolved to establish roots.

Having been released from military service and freed from taxation, the Volkov families became united. Now that they lived next to a military outpost, they were safe from marauding Tatars. The homesteaders prospered once again, and happiness seemed within reach.

These peaceful people became good friends with the border guards. Even though the cavalrymen had their own carpenters, cooks, bakers, smiths, so on and so forth, they prefered to ask the new arrivals to do some chores for the military—things men in uniform don't relish doing, like laundry, baking, mending uniforms, and shoeing horses.

They looked for any pretense just to be with the civilians. The young uniformed men missed their homes and families and wanted to be around peaceable people. However, the elders among the immigrants kept the lonely men at a distance. They warned their young people, especially their daughters, to stay away from the "wicked" non-believers—the smokers, swearers, and drunkards.

Since human beings are gregarious creatures, the barriers that forbade contact between the villagers and the military men, gradually began to crumble. In fact, some young villagers found work at the camp. With time, some of the once homeless border guards began to feel at home among the newcomers. The feeling became mutual with the homesteaders.

Part III

Chapter 7

Stepan Aleksandrovich Volkov

The head of the large Volkov clan was my grandfather, Stepan Aleksandrovich Volkov, the patriarch. He was the chief executive officer of the family. He made all the rules and decisions. He punished the guilty and pardoned the "innocent."

He was very strict about family worship including the Fourth Commandment: no one was to go to the fields without first saying a prayer. And on Sabbaths (Saturdays) no one worked, not even the animals, because riding a horse was considered work for the animal. He followed this Commandment religiously which states in part, "neither your cattle." Stepan considered the word "cattle" to include draft animals.

In his later years, Grandpa Stepan became a cobbler. The Volkovs built a large house to accommodate five families. Besides taking care of house chores, the women worked side by side with their husbands, especially during sowing, planting, and harvesting. Grandpa Stepan was creative when it came to making work easier. As I'd mentioned, my uncles returned home from the military service. Soon, the house was filled with crying babies. While the mothers were in the fields with their husbands, Grandpa became the babysitter.

He made for each infant a swinging cradle. Then, he suspended all the cradles on the rafters, and connected them with cords. One loose cord he extended to his workbench. When one baby cried, he pulled the cord by his foot causing the rest of the cradles to swing while he continued cobbling.

The older children usually played outside, weather permitting. Grandpa was a patient person. He put up with children's noise and let them play, but when a discord erupted among his brood that lead to a physical combat, Grandpa-judge appeared as a "peacemaker."

He had a simple solution for conflict resolution. When he could not determine who the aggressors and who the victims were, he would punish them all. "Go stand in various corners, and don't you dare make a peep until I'm ready to dismiss you."

Children learned fast. No one wanted to be punished without a cause. So as soon as a serious confrontation was about to explode, an informant would speed up before the judge with the news of conflict. Sometimes this method worked and sometimes it backfired. Children learned soon that it was better to endure the pain or an insult than stand in the corner without participating in the melee.

Stepan Aleksandrovich Volkov, the patriarch.

Chapter 8

Grandma Volkov

Grandma Volkov, Fenya Fadeyevna, was a gifted woman. She had a talent in healing. She could diagnose and cure almost any disease at that time and place. She could treat and repair injuries, and deliver babies. She hardly ever stayed home, always attending to a patient in some village, regardless of race or religion.

One time, a group of Tatars from the mountains appeared on horseback at the Volkovs' house in the middle of the night. It had to be at night because they were afraid of the Russian border guards. They put Grandma on horseback and sped back to the mountains.

By morning, the news had spread through Prokhladnoye, "Our doctor has been abducted by Tatars during the night!" In no time, the men of the village appeared on horses before the Volkovs' house with axes, pitchforks, scythes, and clubs to rescue Grandma.

Grandpa came out of the house as cool as could be and asked, "Мужики (Muzhiki, which means men and husbands), what's all this? What do you want?"

"Where is Fenya Fadeyevna?"

"I don't know."

"What do you mean you don't know? You should know exactly where she is! Don't you care?"

"Men, go home. Nothing dreadful will happen. She's not a girl. She can take care of herself. She'll be back, safe and sound. I assure you."

"At least tell us what happened."

"Some Tatars came after her last night and took her with them. Apparently, they need her there. Now go home."

Three nights later, the Tatars returned Grandma with a lamb as payment for her service. Come to find out, the khan's (chieftain's) wife had a complicated childbirth, and the local midwife couldn't deliver the child. The Tatars had heard of our famous "physician" and decided to fetch her for their need. The delivery was successful, mother and child were saved. The khan kept her for two more days to prevent possible complications. During those days, Grandma nursed the mother to health. For her services, the khan offered the "physician" a lamb.

After the wild Tatars returned Grandma at night without harm, Grandpa felt concerned. The child delivery was successful, and Grandma was safe—for the time being. Suppose something similar took place in the future and Grandma wasn't able to save the life of the patient, then what? Grandpa wasn't going to wait for a similar kidnapping to take place. He ordered his clan to pack up all their belongings. They were to move to the Stavropol region in the Northern Caucasus. Grandma continued with her medical skills throughout that region.

In 1916, there was an epidemic of typhus (WP), and Grandma moved from one village to another taking care of the sick. Then, tragedy struck. One day, some villagers brought Fenya Fadeyevna back home, in a wagon—dead from typhus.

✻   ✻   ✻

People began fleeing from large cities, seeking shelter in the countryside and in smaller cities along the peripheries of the nation.

Grandpa Stepan Aleksandrovich followed suit. He considered facing the Tatars posed less danger than the enraged revolutionaries. His darling doctor was dead. Life in Stavropol was precarious. So he rounded up his family, once again. The Volkovs loaded their chattel and trekked back to Turkmenistan.

Chapter 9

Avdotya Afanasievna Koshmina

A mysterious woman appeared in Prokhladnoye. No one knew of her background, where she came from, and why she appeared, of all places, in Prokhladnoye. She didn't broadcast her private life. She only appeared, and was quickly deemed of questionable reputation.

Her name was Avdotya Afanasievna Koshmina. She was of Ukrainian descent, and soon the villagers began to call her khokhlushka (хохлушка), a slightly derogatory term for a Ukrainian woman. For some reason, the Russian "aristocrats" looked down upon the Ukrainians. However, these villagers looked up to this race of people with admiration.

Avdotya was a very intelligent, fun-loving, athletic woman. She had a unique gift, a magnetic personality that appealed especially to the young people. She loved practical jokes. She had a house where she used to throw fun parties for the young people—of course, against the will of the elders of Prokhladnoye. These young people sought her advice relating their innocent amours, and she became a confidante to the bashful youth as a matchmaker.

When we do not have answers for things we don't understand, we tend to fabricate our own, with a lot of color. That's what happened with Avdotya. One such fabrication narrates that on one rainy night, she was returning home from a drinking party with some men. On the way, they had to cross a rivulet. She slipped and fell into this stream. The "gentlemen," instead of rescuing her from the ditch, used her as a stepping stone, and then they pulled her out and dragged her home. So the story goes.

One night, Stepan Aleksandrovich, the widowed patriarch of the Volkov clan, had a vivid dream. He was instructed to go to this questionable "foreigner" and make a marriage proposal to her. Imagine the shock the patriarch experienced in the morning. The dream was persistent. After the third such dream, he decided that it was from God.

So, one day he attired himself in his holiday outfit, combed his beard, rubbed some goose fat on his hair to keep it in place, and trudged timorously toward his dreadful destiny.

He knocked timidly on her door. Then he heard a honey voice say, "Come in." He gingerly crossed the threshold into her den, looking embarrassed and confused. The house was neat and cheerful. Avdotya welcomed him as if she had expected him.

"Welcome, Stepan Aleksandrovich." She offered him a seat. "What can I do for you?" she added.

The discombobulated groom obeyed the command. Clearing his throat, he stuttered, "I came to you on a business proposition."

"What kind of business is that?" she queried.

After an awkward pause, he uttered, "I had a dream that came to me three different times directing me to do something that is contrary to all that I believe in." He stopped, took a deep breath, and, forcing himself, he mumbled sheepishly, "To make a marriage proposal to you." There. He finally verbalized his thoughts, and didn't know what else to add.

The decisive bride came to the point without any hesitation. "Well, Stepan Aleksandrovich, what took you so long? I have been expecting you for some time. I had a similar dream, that you would come to me with the proposal of marriage and that I should accept it."

A thunderclap out of the blue! Poor Stepan, he was on the verge of cardiac arrest.

After the agonizing experience and regaining their composure, they had tea—not champagne. That was the short and the long of it. I don't know the details of their wedding. I can hear the reaction of the community—the jokes, the jeers, and the greasy gossip. Imagine a religious patriarch marrying a stranger with questionable reputation!

Avdotya Afanasievna made a radical reversal of her previous life. In fact, she became a doting wife. Whereas, his previous wife always stayed away from home on rescue missions, this one showered her groom with annoying affection. Grandpa wasn't used to such doting, and awkwardly he would say, "Stop hovering over me!"

In no time, the new Grandma ingratiated herself into the hearts of her "grandchildren" as if they were a mandate from Heaven. She gave them quality attention, allowing Stepan uninterrupted, peaceful time to do his cobbling. This Super Grandma had a most gentle heart. When some recalcitrant cherub needed correction, she applied her *chepchik* (bonnet) on his or her behind, and then asked him or her, "Did I hurt you?"

After the initial shock of the bizarre marriage, people in the community began to accept this state of affairs. Her status in society rose from a woman in the gutter to a lady of honor. The lovesick village youth resumed their trek to the doorsteps of this loving and loveable "Grandma."

Avdotya must have been quite an athlete in her younger days. Shortly after she married Stepan Aleksandrovich, a group of people went out for an outing of sorts. It must have been some holiday. The day was warm, and some brave broods decided to cool off in the river. On one side of the riverbank, there happened to be a high rise.

Avdotya Afanasievna announced she wanted to swim, too. Quite a shocking announcement! Some curious kids wanted to see the show—a grandmother swimming in the river. But, she did not go to the gentle slope where the children and the timid went.

She headed for the steep bank. She did some stretches and unexpectedly plunged in. Everyone dashed to see a granny surface, but granny was nowhere to be seen. They waited and waited, but not even a bubble surfaced. Panic ensued. People herded to the high bank and peered into the deep. No grandmother. A command was issued for the daring young men to dive into the river and find the drowned woman. Several brave men dared to dive.

When the men surfaced from the bottom of the river, they saw her sitting on the ledge of the steep bank shouting to them, "What are you searching for? Have you found anything?" There was a lot of hilarity and shaking of heads.

I vaguely remember her as a resolute, toothless old woman. She used to carry pincers in her long wide skirt pocket for cracking lumped sugar. In those days, sugar came in pyramid shape. People used to break the pyramid sugar with an ax or a hammer into smaller lumps, and then bite into yet smaller pieces. Since my step-grandmother had no teeth, she resorted to the pincers. People claimed she lived to be 104 years old.

Avdotya Afanasievna (Koshmina) Volkov.

Chapter 10

Vasiliy Stepanovich Volkov

Although, these immigrants were coping with their complicated lives, their trust in God grew stronger. Some continued searching the Bible for further truths. My uncle, Vasiliy Stepanovich Volkov, was one of them. He and a friend began to study the New Testament in earnest. In doing so, they came to the subject of baptism by immersion and its meaning. No church, no pastor, just God.

They became convinced of its importance. However, the question arose of how to go about it and who to do the baptizing. To seek a solution to their problem, they turned to God for guidance. He had impressed on them that they should confess their sins to Him and then be baptized, but how? Another question arose, who is to baptize whom first. Neither one of them dared to perform this solemn rite.

They decided to approach God once again for their pressing question. They found a secluded place by the river, knelt on the riverbank, and prayed. They were impressed to draw lots. After the decision was confirmed by lottery, they took their clothes off and stepped into the water. Following the baptism, they stepped out of the water, dressed, and headed home in deep contemplative silence.

Soon after this awesome act, some Seventh-day Adventist missionaries arrived to their village with additional Biblical truths. The two baptized friends attended the study meetings and accepted the additional Biblical messages. When the preacher spoke about baptism, the two friends explained their experience at the riverbank.

After the missionaries quizzed them on the meaning of baptism, they were convinced that Vasiliy and his friend understood the meaning of baptism correctly. They accepted the two friends into the Adventist communion on the profession of their faith, without being rebaptized.

During this religious study, at least two families accepted Adventism, the Bakholdins and the Muravyovs. It wasn't that they changed their faith, they just added new message to, and expanded the meaning of, what they had already believed.

✳ ✳ ✳

However, the controversy between God and Satan over these simple people was not over. When a person surrenders his or her life to God, that's when Satan summons his mighty forces against the children of God.

And so it was with Uncle Vasiliy Stepanovich. His wife, Maria Borisovna (Aunt Masha), became mentally ill. She turned quiet and fearful, and often carried conversation with invisible beings. She took good care of her family, physically. Years of routine housework became mechanical. Cooking, cleaning, washing, and the like, continued without interruption.

Although she was a gentle, honest, caring woman, she lost contact with adults. She could not carry rational conversation. She was locked in her own private world, and no one could unlock it. Some people could not understand Aunt Masha's condition, so they wove about it their own convoluted ideas and passed them on to others until gossip was accepted as fact. Meanwhile, the poor woman suffered. Others who refused to accept the gossip tried to help materially, but that was not what she needed, so they too gave up. Some were even afraid of her. Even her husband lost contact with her.

To complicate this family's ordeal, their eldest son—with a great musical gift many lusted after—drowned in a river. It was too much for Uncle Vasiliy to bear. He stopped attending church services, and eventually took to drinking. As if that wasn't enough, one time in our village, Rahmatabad, Uncle Vasiliy went to the neighboring forest for firewood. While chopping wood, he encountered a black bear. There was a skirmish between the two. The beast got the better of the man with his axe and left him wounded.

Because the scuffle was close to our house, Uncle Vasiliy shouted for help. My sister Nadya heard her uncle's plea. She asked Batya (father) to listen carefully. Sure enough, he heard a faint call from his brother, "Isay! Isay!"

Immediately, he summoned some men, and they responded to the call. They found him bleeding. The men constructed a makeshift stretcher and brought the wounded patient to our house.

Eventually, his wounds healed, and he was able to resume his daily activities, though with some limitation. Not long after the attack, Vasiliy died, leaving behind his helpless wife and two sons. Shortly thereafter, Aunt Masha passed away too. Their two sons, Ivan and Vladimir, became orphaned. The older, Ivan, was only a teenager. He hired himself out to various people as a helping hand. Vladimir, the younger son, lived as a foster child among relatives.

Both brothers grew up to be successful additions to society and active participants in religious activities. Later, Ivan became a taxi driver in the capital of Iran, Tehran. After emigration to America, he became a farmer and a successful storeowner in Kerman, California. Vladimir married a Baptist girl and accepted his wife's religion. One of their children, a son, had a gift for poetry.

Part IV

Chapter II

Communism Spreads

Through successful propaganda, Communism spread rapidly tightening its grip on diversified cultures—in spite of the vastness in territory of the Russian empire. Like a cancer, its incubation started in large cities. From there, its viral tentacles spread to the peripheries of the country, small towns and villages.

The communists inculcated their ideologies by convincing people of the glorious advantages of their regime. In rural areas, however, they minimized the ideology. Instead, they attracted the simple people with folk art and music, and brute force. They reached the darkest communities with their portable cinematography, choral works, live or recorded, and dance groups.

No doubt some of you older Americans have seen such dance, choral, civilian, and military troupes, and have watched their movies in theaters in America. Their entertaining organizations were so good that they traveled around the world. Their ballet and Olympic programs were famous worldwide. Under Communism, the entertainment program had one purpose: glorification of Communism. I'll mention one movie, Wedding in Malinovka (Свадьба в Малиновке), a perfect example of crass Soviet propaganda. The setting of the movie is a village called, Malinovka. It features humor, drama, romance, and folk music. In it, the villagers are portrayed as pleasant, decent simple people. On the other hand, the czarists (previous regime) were pictured as repulsive, crude, cruel clowns—even in their attire.

To disseminate their propaganda effectively, the Soviets "electrified" small towns and rural communities by building dams and powerhouses throughout all fifteen republics. Under Communism, the first priority went to the military. The second, to exportation of performing arts. Citizens, however, came last.

*   *   *

While the war raged on in the interior areas, we who lived along the peripheries of the country were left alone—for the time being. While the population of the interior was starving and dying, we, on the border of Persia, were temporarily "forgotten," though not for long.

Our only suffering was in sending our wheat to the government to feed starving citizenry in the heart of Russia. We, on the other hand, had to settle for barley bread. To us, barley was considered food for animals. Little did we know, barley is just as nutritious as wheat, if not more so.

The political plague finally reached us on the edges of the young Communist country.

One day, a communist official, Borisov, appeared at our village with his deputies. Borisov was notorious for convincing peasants to form collective (government) farms. On the success of his previous conquests, he anticipated quick attainment of his goals.

Elders of the Prokhladnoye families had been expecting such a visit, and now it arrived. Borisov asked village leaders to assemble a meeting in the village school. After a friendly icebreaker, he painted a glorious future in Communism. The very first thing the elders posed to him was, "We have been promised freedom from taxes, military draft, and government interference in our lives for fifteen years. That time has not expired yet."

"That was promised by the old Czarist repressive regime, which is nullified now. This is a new, friendly government and has its own rules, laws, and regulations," promptly retorted Borisov. The men looked at each other nervously. Then, one of them stood up and said, "Comrade Borisov, please give us some time so we can get our thoughts together."

After a long pause, Borisov gave his answer. "Alright, I'll give you two weeks. Be sure you give me a definite answer when I return, and I hope it will be a positive one." The meeting was dismissed.

The very next day, the heads of families of Prokhladnoye and Silukli assembled in a building where they conducted worship services. The men were quiet and somber. The meeting started with a prayer. They all knew that forming a collective farm was out of the question. Such an act would lead to losing their freedom to conduct their own affairs, especially the freedom of worship. They well knew the power of Borisov and his cruel tactics. The pressing question was what to do about it? What action to take? They decided to approach the heavenly Counselor, Who had led them in the past. They knelt to pray.

It's interesting to note that even in peaceful circumstances there was discord, conflict, competition, and jealousy among the villagers, but under a grave concern and common threat— all these differences evaporated. With one accord, they all agreed to confess their sins before God. They also asked each other to forgive their own offenses against one another and promised to right the wrongs. They appointed a period of prayer and fasting. In two days, they were to assemble again and bring their ideas on what course of action to pursue.

The elders of Prokhladnoye assembled once again to make final decisions on how to proceed with new developments. After hearing various opinions and long deliberation, they decided to put their plan into action: 1) Send scouts to Persia to request asylum. The committee chose Stepan Kaptsov, avid hunter, and my uncle, Aleksey Volkov, since both spoke some Farsi; 2) Carry on with daily activities to appear normal; 3) Ask Borisov to give them another postponement; 4) Watch the activities of the military outpost; 5) Prepare a route for escape; 6) All the horses were to be well shoed and well cared for, and wagons repaired; 7) Decide how to drive the cattle across the border; 8) Above all, keep their plans top secret, even from family members; 9) Continue praying.

The scouts were dispatched. After long and agonizing anticipation, they returned from Persia. Members of the secret committee assembled to hear the report. The scouts said that they had to bribe the Persian border guards to make a deal.

When the elders heard about the bribe, they were quite concerned. They knew that people who accept bribes are not dependable. What would prevent the Persian border guards from accepting a more profitable bribe and reneging on their promise of security for the refugees? A risky proposition. They had no choice. The only option was to trust God.

Another great concern was the time factor with pressure from Borisov, who insisted on immediate submission to his "proposal." He had perfected his means of operation in attaining his desired end, and did not want his mission to miscarry while he was on top of his career.

They were apprehensive about their plans of escape. If discovered, they may lose everything—including their lives. There were a few members in the community with loose lips. However, some were on chummy relations with the neighboring soldiers. After long deliberation over their dilemma, the elders made their final decision—escape to Persia, and petition to Providence.

Chapter 12

The Die Is Cast

Now, before them lay the most frightening trial of their lives: how to orchestrate their flight to Persia without raising suspicion of the border militia and Borisov. Most crucial elements of their plan were time, speed, and security. They realized the enormity of their decision. They also realized that without a miracle they would perish.

After lengthy silence and deep sighs, they knelt and with heavy hearts, pleaded with God for protection, guidance, strength, and wisdom. They ended their plea with reciting Psalms 91 and 121. They stressed passages such as, "*"He* is my refuge and my fortress; my God, in Him I will trust...For He shall give His angels charge over you to keep you in all your ways."' They cited God's message, "He shall call upon Me, and I will answer him; I *will be* with him in trouble; I will deliver him and honor him."'

Prayers said, they remained on their knees, feeling that they had overlooked something, something else they could have added to their prayers. Finally, they rose to their feet. According to their custom, they embraced and kissed each other. They agreed to fast the next day. Despite their fears of breaching security, they decided to reveal their crucial crisis to some of their trusted family members. They swore their families to secrecy. It was deep in the night as each man with heavy heart trod slowly toward his home.

The following evening, the men assembled again and began their deliberations with a fervent prayer. They nominated grandfather, Stepan Aleksandrovich, as their representative. Utmost on their agenda was to appoint some dependable young men to prepare the route of escape: trees to be felled, brush to be cleared, rocks and logs to be removed, ditches to be filled, because they had to travel through wooded and hilly terrain.

At the end of each day as they returned from the woods, they had to bring something in their wagons, either firewood or some logs. Spending a whole day in the forest with tools and returning home empty would definitely look suspicious.

The rest were to continue doing whatever they did at that time of the year, which was spring, a time for cultivating the soil and planting seeds. They had to act surreptitiously, because almost on a daily basis someone from the military base would come to Prokhladnoye either on some small business or just to "kill" the boring free time. In such cases, the elders spent their clandestine sessions deep into the night. One time, one of the soldiers, noticing the light in the "church" commented, "Why do you have worship service every night?"

That comment put the elders in real concern. They decided to entertain the unwanted guests far away from their meeting place and be generous with potent brew which they kept for medicinal purpose. Meanwhile, they elicited vital information from their "guests" about the camp's activities. The vodka served a vital purpose—medicine and security.

They also worried about provisions; after all, they needed food to survive in an unknown place. To provide for subsistence, they slaughtered chickens and lambs, fried their meat and placed it in crocks; after that, they covered the contents with melted sheep tail fat. This content was called *ghuyurma*. This way the meat could last for years without spoiling, especially when it was buried in the ground.

Before long, Borisov showed up unexpectedly and demanded their decision. When the elders pleaded for more time, Borisov lost his temper. He shouted, "Don't play games with me! I am not to be trifled with. Either you submit to the government demands peacefully or you will be disfranchised. In that case you will be treated as enemies of the state."

Neither was a desirable proposition. To these humble people it meant loss of their religious freedom or death sentence in Siberia.

Like the old Pharaoh of Egypt, Borisov threatened, "When I return," Borisov added, "I'll come with military force and deal with you according to our law." And he stormed off in a huff. That threat really intensified the already unbearable stress and fear among the people. They were on the point of panic.

Chapter 13

Isay Stepanovich Volkov

My father, Isay (ee-SAHY, Isaiah)—we called him Batya, an old form for father—never liked farming. He preferred city life, so he settled in Ashkhabad, not far from Prokhladnoye. He found himself a job on the railroad as a switchman.

Later, when Communism reached the capital, Batya was appointed secretary of the local government. He was urged to join the Communist party, but he refused. However, because of his good work ethic and because Communism was in the fluid state, they overlooked his objection and kept him on the job for a while.

Eventually, life became good—for that time and place. In fact, on September 30, 1928, he wrote a letter to his brother-in-law, Vasiliy Sevastyanovich Kosarev, in America, stating that the family had 3 cows, 6 calves, 17 goats, and about 50 chickens. Their oldest son, Aleksey, 19, was given a job at the railroad. Their oldest daughter, Manya (Margarita),

17, was working in an office. Anna was finishing high school. Life looked good.

Then one day a messenger arrived for Batya with urgent, top-secret news: "pack up immediately and move to Prokhladnoye with all your family. We are escaping to Persia."

This bit of news was upsetting to Batya. He declined the "invitation." But, the messenger was instructed to convince him to follow through with the "order" at all cost.

The messenger stressed, "You have no choice, Isay Stepanovich. Your father insists that you follow the orders."

"All the villagers are farmers," responded Batya, "they can survive anywhere. I am not a farmer and don't want to be one."

"There are several reasons for you to join the family," insisted the messenger." You have seven children. Some of them are of marriageable age. Whom are they going to marry, the godless communists? Besides, what do you think will happen to you and your family, when Borisov pops up and sees that all your family has disappeared? Your children will become wards of the state, and you and your wife will be sent to Siberia. Just think about it. It's a serious situation."

"You're right there," yielded Batya unwillingly. "Still, I must discuss this matter with my wife."

"I'm sure she will see my point. I know a mother's heart when it comes to her children. Don't delay. Time is of the essence. So long. God be with you." They parted.

That night, Batya confided the news to Mama. Mama was a brave, resolute, fearless woman. She had great perception. After hearing the shocking news, she acted quickly. She was ready to pack up that moment.

Later that night, they sought guidance from God, pleading for wisdom and protection. Finally, they decided to pack up and leave. They spent the sleepless night devising a plan of informing the authorities of their sudden move. First, they decided to reveal their secret only to Manya, making her swear to total secrecy of their decision.

The problem was this: Batya, their oldest son, Aleksey, and oldest daughter, Manya (Maria, later Margarita), were employed by the Communist Party. One daughter, Anna, was in a government boarding school, and two were in regular school. They couldn't just pack up and disappear. They had to give some plausible explanation for their sudden departure. They had to be very careful of what to say. Any careless word could have jeopardized their safety

It was Manya's responsibility to talk her younger sister, Anna, to take a "short leave of absence" from her studies because of some emergencies with their grandparents. She had to do it in such a way so not to raise any suspicions. Manya had a hard time convincing Anna to go to Prokhladnoye. When presented with an ultimatum, Anna pleaded, "At least let me tell my friends goodbye." Any means of alerting the authorities was what my parents feared most. After some confrontation, Anna yielded with a lot of grumbling.

Manya was the oldest daughter in the family. Reading and writing came easy for her. In fact, she was Batya's favorite child. Quite often, on free days, he would ask her to read something for him, and she complied happily.

Batya just told his "employers" that he had to join the rest of the family in Prokhladnoye, because there were some serious family problems.

Finally, they loaded their wagon, tied their prized cow to it, and headed to the uncertain, risky future. Batya grumbled the whole way. The family consisted of nine members: the parents, their oldest son, Aleksey, Margarita, Anna, Michael, Tatyana (Tanya), Nadezhda (Nadya), and baby Yakov (the author) who wasn't even one-year-old.

The younger children were quite bewildered of this strange upsetting of their lives. Father and the three older siblings were beside themselves. Batya and Aleksey were working at the railroad station,

Margarita was working in the office and loving it. Anna was in high school enjoying life with many of her fun-loving friends.

None of them wanted to exchange their "happy" life for some unknown foreign, unchristian country. In fact, my parents agreed to keep Anna in the dark from the real situation. Batya didn't have the heart to deal with Anna. He repined the whole time, so he delegated this responsibility to Margarita. Anna was not going to abandon her friends, even when she was presented with an ultimatum.

Mama, however, was ready to go to the extreme for the sake of her children's future happiness. She saw turbulent signs in her country and sensed the ominous future that boded nothing but pain and suffering for them. She was a deeply religious woman. She trusted God; that He would take care of them the way He had done so in the past.

She hadn't forgotten her father's trust in God, and the visions he had received from Above, and how miraculously God delivered them from various trials.

While the rest fretted and moaned, Mama kept reminding them of God's blessings in the past. She was a tenacious woman, able to allay her husband's fears and encourage him to go through with their dreadful decision. Little by little,

Batya quieted down, and they all arrived safely to Prokhladnoye. The whole Volkov family was at last intact.

As Batya entered the Prokhladnoye house, he was shocked to see that most of their household things were already packed. Batya blew up.

"Where do you think you're going?" He added sarcastically, "Do you expect the military outpost to escort you wherever you plan to go?"

"Keep your voice down," responded his father, Stepan Aleksandrovich, calmly." We have already made arrangements with the Persian border guards to give us free passage to Persia, and we're waiting for an opportune time."

"Do you realize what you're saying?" fumed Batya with an even louder voice." This is suicide!"

Chapter 14

The Crisis

No sooner had my family arrived in Prokhlad-noye to join the rest of the family, than did Borisov and his deputies appear on their doorsteps. He arrived with papers to finalize any discussions and organize the collective farm, calling for a meeting at once. He was there to terminate further deliberation, and to commence collectivization.

At the meeting, Stepan Aleksandrovich spoke. "Comrade Borisov, we are not quite ready at this moment for such an act..." But, before the spokesman finished his speech, Borisov became irate and barked out, "No more games! You had your chances! I was patient with you, but enough is enough! Don't you realize you have no choice in this matter! This is not a business transaction! No more haggling! Whatever agreement you had with the previous regime is now void. I have come to the end of my patience." He then turned to one of his deputies and ordered, "Sergey, get the papers and put them on the table." Then, turning to Stepan, he commanded, "Sign this document!"

The elders were transfixed. Nobody moved. The representative uttered, "We can't."

Borisov's face turned crimson. He exploded, "You are all disfranchised! You are no longer our citizens. You are now enemies of our country. Next week, I'm bringing a military detachment. Your property will be confiscated, and you will be exiled! It could be Siberia!" At the end of his tirade, he ordered his deputies to depart from the premises. They all stormed out with a huff, rendering the elders speechless.

After a long silence, one of the elders spoke, "Men, what now?" Solemn silence ensued. Then, Grandfather Stepan Volkov spoke, "*Muzhiki*, (men, husbands), we are not totally hopeless. Let's not forget our God. He has led us in the past, and He'll provide a way of escape now. Let us turn to Him for help."

The elders knelt, and Stepan offered a heartrending prayer with tears. His was not the only teary face.

No sooner had the elders risen from their knees, than someone burst into the meeting place uttering, "They're gone! They're gone!"

"Who's gone? Calm down. Talk plainly."

All the elders surrounded the excited messenger in alarm." Sit down, relax, talk slowly," repeated Stepan calmly and deliberately.

"The border guards. They're all gone, except two of them."

"Did you talk to them?"

"Yes."

"What did they say?"

"They said that there's a big contraband crossing the border into Russia and our guards went to intercept them."

"Men, do you realize what this means?" Now, Stepan himself became excited." God answered our prayers before we even asked Him!" he exclaimed. This is the window of opportunity we have been praying for!"

"Praise God! Praise His name! Now what?"

"'Now what?!'" repeated Stepan with a raised voice. "Load up the wagons and move," he added.

Chapter 15

The Exodus

The elders knelt again and lifted their voices to God. This time it was with tears of joy, not apprehension. Now that they received the desired answer to their prayers, they pleaded for guidance. After rising from their knees, they sprang into action. They asked David Popov (not his real name), a villager with dubious morals who worked at the military outfit, to do what he deemed necessary.

He was to keep the two guards in total ignorance of the villagers' plans, and the meaning of the commotion that was about to take place. Popov couldn't dream of a better assignment. He knew exactly what he was supposed to do—and *this* he would enjoy doing. He was going to have a drinking party with the blessing of the elders. Besides, he had his own devious plans.

Without losing any precious time, the elders decided to begin their exodus the following night, no matter what. They had only one day to pack.

The elders chose a young alert man of action to mount a horse and gallop through the Prokhladnoye and Selyukli villages, proclaiming deliverance. With the utmost urgency and caution, they were to load their wagons with all their possessions and get ready to head for Persia within 24 hours. The elders asked Stepan Kaptsov and Aleksey Stepanovich Volkov, the two scouts who had bribed the Persian border guards to accept the Russian refugees. They were to inform the Persian guards to expect the fleeing refugees the following night. Early in the morning, the scouts were on their way.

The elders also asked their Russian-speaking Persian herdsman to organize a group of young people to help him drive their cattle across the border. For his services, they promised to reward him generously. They also instructed him to have all the grain bins opened to feed the cattle with that precious grain; after all, it had to be abandoned. The long expectant night had arrived—the window of opportunity they were praying for flung widely ajar. It came suddenly, unexpectedly. It brought joy mixed with terrifying fear of the unknown, yet with hope.

The frantic packing and loading commenced. Even though most of the families had been forewarned of this event, no one really knew when, and *if* this event would even take place. Some took the warning seriously and started packing the necessary possessions immediately.

Others procrastinated, or questioned such a possibility, and were caught by surprise. And now, panic-stricken, they began to stuff their chattel helter-skelter. The wise ones packed—besides their provisions—even seeds for vegetables, flowers, and grain. Some took along children's books and primers. Religious materials were neatly packed with the utmost care.

Batya grudgingly reconciled himself to the urgency of the matter and realized the impossibility of reversing the flow of the event. Therefore, he helped Mama with swift, diligent care of preparations to flee. He sensed the enormity of the situation and decided to record this historic move in a diary for posterity; after all, he had served as a secretary of the City Council. In his diary, he listed members of each family by age, as far as he could determine their ages, as no one recorded birth, marriage, and death events. Calendars were unknown. They kept the record based on natural and political events, such as droughts, floods, and other natural disasters. Other events, such as widely known births, deaths, coronations and assassinations of royalties and political leaders, served as date markers.

In the village lived a couple of childless Communist schoolteachers. The elders asked them to join them and continue their teaching profession in Persia. However, they refused. "We are not one of your people," they said. "What will happen to us when we become old and infirm; who will take care of us?" They were promised love and to be cared for, but they remained adamant about staying and promised that they would not betray the elders. "Go with your God," they said. "We wish you a safe journey and happiness."

The crescent of the moon had just hidden behind the horizon. Darkness set in. The harried commotion of loading possessions had begun. Those who had anticipated such events, and had packed necessary items in advance, began loading things in orderly fashion. Others who had procrastinated found themselves in a confused situation, and madly began to throw their chattel in disorderly assemblage into the wagons. My youngest uncle's family was already on the move when they discovered that in the moment of frenzy and commotion they had left their infant daughter, Nadya, behind. My uncle, Fyodor Volkov (he had previously served in a cavalry regiment), turned his steed around and galloped on horseback to rescue his daughter. He returned in no time, cradle in hand, with Nadya in it.

After the mad rush was over, the villagers—as they had practiced in their custom for generations—knelt in a circle and pleaded with God to send them guardian angels to accompany them on this momentous exodus.

With every member of the family aboard their wagon, Batya, being somewhat of a romantic walked back into the house. He wound the wall chime clock and placed the key on top of it. He tapped the clock gently and walked out of the house. The clock struck twelve midnight, he briefly froze. He took a deep breath, and shrugging, waved his hand backward, walking away with rapid pace. The date was Wednesday, May 13, 1931.

✳   ✳   ✳

My cousin Faina (Fenya) and her family were inadvertently left behind. They lived in Bakharden some 65 miles east of Ashkhabad. Besides, Faina's brother belonged to a Communist youth organization, Komsomol. This painful decision was necessary to avoid jeopardizing the safety of the rest of the families.

Years later, in 1964, Faina was invited to visit us in America. She told us of what she had witnessed after the villages were abandoned. She said that the shocking news of her relatives escaping into

Persia had reached her and her family a couple of days later. They decided to find out for themselves.

When they arrived at Prokhladnoye, they witnessed a heartrending, surrealistic scene. It was apocalyptic. The first thing that struck them was the mourning howls of the dogs. Ghostly, yawning empty houses, hens sitting on eggs in nests, and one solitary cow (Batya's prized animal)—paralyzed their sense of reality. This scene was so shocking that they cried for days.

Because the flight was so urgent and sudden, additional relatives in other places were also left behind. Some of my Volkov cousins who lived in Ashkhabad were uninformed. Vasiliy Trafimovich Konovalov's wife, Fenya Trafimovna, was away from home at the time and was also left behind. Later, Vasiliy slipped into the Soviet Union and brought her safely back across the border.

This was not an isolated incident. Vasiliy Grigorievich Loskutov, who joined us later on in Rahmatabad, left his whole family in Russia. And much later, Ivan Zenoveyevich Gorbenko joined us, too, with his two sons, Pavel and Gregoriy, leaving the rest of the family in Ukraine.

My brother-in-law to be, Nikolay Terentievich Osadtchi, a university student at the time, was being transported by train, headed for a Siberian labor camp. He jumped off the train into a river below as the train crossed a bridge. He never learned of the plight of his wealthy, aristocratic family back home in Ukraine.

He later married my young and widowed sister, Margarita. They had three children: Igor, Olga, and Oleg. A gifted engineer, Nikolay built two mills in the city of Qazvin in Persia. Soon after that, the city hired him to build an electric station. Because of his engineering genius, every home in the city was wired for electricity.

Olga, Margarita, Nikolay, and Igor Osadtchi.

☆   ☆   ☆

David Popov completed his assignment with superb mastery. He intoxicated the two guards to oblivion. He then chose the guards' best team of workhorses, selected their sturdiest wagon (these were Communist property), galloped home, loaded his chattel, and joined the rest of the fleeing caravan.

The exodus was miraculous. In all this commotion, in the darkness of night and crossing the wooded hills, the flight was successful. The men who had prepared the route of escape led the procession. Only the infirm and very young rode on wagons; the rest walked.

Mothers were strictly instructed to keep their infants quiet. To accomplish that, some mothers rubbed their nipples with opium and nursed their young ones. Some refused to resort to drugging their infants, so instead, they nursed their darlings constantly, whether they needed it or not. In some cases, pillows served the purpose of maintaining the silence—taking precautions not to suffocate their nurslings, of course.

The village shepherd followed the elders' charge. He rounded the teenagers, including the girls, and ordered them to drive the cattle following the caravan. This procession was so successful that only one stubborn cow returned to the village, and that was our prized bovine. She was as unwilling to leave her home as her master was. Batya called her "the Communist Sympathizer." Surprisingly, more animals were not lost in the darkness.

Part V

Chapter 16

On Persian Territory

As planned, and with God's help, the refugees crossed through wooded hills and entered Persian territory. The sun had just risen. The fleeing families knelt down and lifted their gratitude to God, Who had led them safely to this new land. The Persian border guards welcomed them graciously.

Some sharp-eyed individuals looked back at the hills they had crossed during the night. They noticed the Soviet border guards racing on their horses along the clearing on the hilltop up above. The refugees were alarmed. Once their friends and protectors, now their enraged enemies might cross the border and force them back to Soviet Russia. Thankfully, that didn't happen–not yet.

Though the fugitives were somewhat safe in Persia, they were still on private property which belonged to a very rich and influential warlord. The Persian border guards had informed the warlord of these families who had entered his land from Russia.

The property owner instructed them to select a place on his territory for the runaways on a temporary basis. So the refuge seekers settled in a place called Kuly (koo-lee), close to the border. Those who had tents pitched them. Others excavated crude dugouts in the escarpment for their shelter.

Soon, news of the refugees spread among neighboring villagers. These gracious people came to Kuly with gifts of dried fruit, bread, and assortment of produce. In no time, the runaways settled on a spot the best way the circumstances permitted.

The feudal lord who allowed these Russian trespassers to settle on his territory also kept a harem in his residence. He was known to be cruel and vengeful. One day, this chieftain decided to check out these escapees. He arrived at Kuly in pomp, on horseback and with a delegation of his underlings. It happened to be a sunny day, and a group of girls sat in the meadow singing Russian folk songs. Margarita, Batya's favorite daughter, accompanied them on a guitar.

The harem owner immediately laid his eyes on Margarita. He asked his Russian servant—whose beautiful wife the khan had locked up in his harem—to inquire whose daughter the guitar player was.

The sad subordinate brought the answer.

The khan called for Batya, who was chopping wood. Batya came forward with an axe in his hand. The chieftain asked him through the interpreter, "Is that your daughter?"

Batya surmised where this question led. Bracing himself for the next question, he cautiously answered, "Yes, she is."

"How much do you ask for her?" asked the self-assured harem owner.

It was the wrong question to ask the wrong man in the wrong place at the wrong time. Short-tempered, Batya's blood was already boiling from the bad turn of events. He hated being there, and then being asked to sell the apple of his eye—it was the last straw. He erupted like a cornered grizzly, and, waving the axe, he shouted, "My daughter is not an animal or a thing to be sold or bartered for! Out of my way!"

One dares not insult a ruler with a super ego in front of his underlings, especially when the trespasser is on the ruler's territory. The warlord's bodyguards were about to tear Batya into pieces. Luckily, the master stopped them with a wave of his hand. He just threatened Batya, "You will regret your words," and prodded his steed with his stirrups, trotting away, bodyguards in tow. He too didn't dare to create a tragic scene in front of many witnesses.

After all, there was someone else above him in the government.

The onlookers were aghast at the scene. They were ready to eat Batya alive! Mama put her arm around Batya and led him into the dugout to cool off.

*   *   *

A few days had passed since the audacious incident. The elders noticed that their shepherd drove the cattle home from pasture in haste, much earlier in the day than usual. They sensed some urgency and approached him with questions, "What happened?"

Without answering their query, he just panted, "Men, you have been betrayed. I saw the Russian guards and the Persian border guards holding a meeting today at the border. They parted with handshakes."

The elders' ire riled against Batya.

They assembled in one of the tents for making plans and, once again, cried to God for deliverance. At the meeting, they decided to pack again. However, which direction to flee they could not decide. To the north was the Soviet Union. To the southwest of the foothills stood the Kopet-Dag Mountain Range. The only way they could go was east, along a path that closely paralleled the Soviet border.

The following morning, the commander of the Persian border guards arrived with his attendants and asked for a meeting. The commander ordered the refugees to pack, and during the night move further into the interior of Persia. He ordered them to travel east. The reason for this route, he explained, was that it was easier and closer to the main city. The reason for the move at night, according to border guards, was to not alert the Soviet guards. That sounded logical. However, it presented a trap which they intended to avoid.

Once again, they turned to their Master Guide for the right guidance. God heard their plea and provided them the right guidance. He sent them a human guide, their herdsman. He informed the elders not to take the ordered route, because there will be an ambush of Russian guards. Instead, they were to attempt the mountain range. The problem with this route was not only the steep ascent, but also the loose graveled hills.

Again, they dispatched the two trusted men. Stepan Kaptsov and Aleksey Volkov were to go to the nearest city, where there was a government office. The scouts mounted the fastest horses and galloped for help.

This time, the refugees were not packing their things in secret as before. They worked all day long openly with haste. That was the command. Toward the evening, most every family had their wagons loaded.

As soon as twilight turned to dusk, the frightened people came into action. The moon was half full. One covered wagon was designated for the girls. To keep them out of sight from the khan's underlings, men packed them into the wagon. They covered them with a tarp and ordered them to keep absolute silence, because some bad men were planning to kidnap them and make them slaves.

The arduous task of scrambling up the graveled crest commenced in semidarkness. Wagon by wagon was slowly pulled and pushed upward. Animals pulled and men pushed and groaned. It was easier to accomplish the task when the oxen pulled. They pulled slowly and steadily. The horses, however, tried to scale the ridge with speed by jerking, impeding progress. The situation was frustrated further when one wagon turned over and some of its contents rolled down the hill. It took the refugees the whole night to overcome the crest.

As if this frenzied frustration was not enough, Fenya Kaptsov, Stepan's wife, was attacked by labor pangs. Aunt Anna Danilovna, my Uncle Fyodor's wife, was called to deliver the child. Anna, with other women, led the suffering mother behind some bushes to fend to Fenya's needs. The delivery was successful. It was a boy. He was named Vasiliy Stepanovich Kaptsov. It was July 2, 1931.

The sky was already turning grey—a dawn of a new day. The last wagon reached the crest of the hill. People and animals needed rest.

Just as everyone was about to praise the Lord for overcoming the difficult part of their labor, they saw the commander of the Persian border guards. He was with his retinue on horseback, ascending the mountain with speed, shouting.

Pandemonium broke out. Frightened, exhausted and without sleep, the refugees were primed for panic. As soon as they heard and saw in the early dawn the shouting of the armed border guards, terror took over. The women, as if on command, broke out into a wail like howling of hungry jackals. The children joined in.

The commander of the guards, waving his rifles, ordered everyone to turn around and head into the prescribed direction. Women, clutching their infants, sat on the ground and refused to move. The men stood transfixed.

At the height of confusion, the scouts, with a Russian-speaking government deputy, galloped up to the mountaintop on sweating horses. The women surrounded the official on their knees and pleaded, "Please save us! Rescue us from the Communists."

The government official yelled at the commander of the border guards, "What is going on here?! Explain this scene!"

"These foreigners disobeyed orders to move into the interior of our land," responded the commander.

"What's all this wailing? Why are they on top of this mountain?" raged the government official.

Sensing severe reprisal, the commander added, "I don't really know where they got the idea that Communists are after them."

According to Aunt Anna Danilovna, the midwife, the official got off his horse and approached the commander. He tore the commander's epaulettes off his shoulders and kicked him in the rear; a common practice in the Persian military at that time—justice on the spot. He then turned to the refugees and addressed them in Russian, "Go on your way. You're safe now."

The wailing turned into sniffling, followed by deep sighs of relief. Tragedy averted.

Chapter 17

In the Strange Land

The wanderers descended from the hill on the other side, and temporarily settled in a small valley with their cattle. They were still on private property. Now, they decided to look for a permanent place, where they could live legally.

At that time, Persia was still in the hands of feudal lords. Once again, the refugees dispatched the scouts in search of an appropriate place to stay. They found five feudal warlords who were willing to accept these homeless families. Now before them lay a choice: on whose property to settle. The scouts recommended two sites, one close to their abandoned camp and the other much further west, at the foothills of the Elburz Mountain Range.

After long deliberation, the party split the way they had lived in Turkmenistan. The smaller group opted for the closer territory called, Guledag. The group from Prokhladnoye chose the distant area.

Our family of seven children, however, refused to join either party. They hitched their team of horses to their wagon, loaded their possessions, and headed to a city called Bojnurd. They didn't have to worry about cattle since their only prized stubborn cow had her own idea of independence; just like her master, she refused to belong to anyone.

In Bojnurd, my parents stopped at a *caravanserai*, a type of roadside inn, where they could rent a space for some time. Soon, they found employment as teamsters and decided to stay there as long as they could.

The larger party arrived at their destination and presented themselves to the feudal lord of that area. This warlord, to the amazement of the wayfarers, ordered the residents of one village, called Rahmatabad (meaning Abode of Mercy or "Merciville"), to vacate their homes and disperse among other villages. This act of grace was an indication to the exhausted refugees that they indeed were welcome in this strange land.

Strange as it seemed, the locals showed no animosity, at least overtly, towards the Russians; throughout the whole time the Russians lived there, over some twenty years. There was one family that refused to move, they had the best house on the edge of the village.

The warlord gave these foreigners not only a village, but also all the land they could till. The landowner required 1/8 of their main crop, mostly wheat. Unlike the Israelites' struggle for land in Canaan, these refugees did not even beg or fight for receiving such graciousness. On top of that, the warlord loaned them some means to establish themselves.

For the first time in their lives, these people felt no fear or pressure from anyone including interference with their religious practices. In addition, being stateless, their young men were not subject to military draft or government taxes, except what they owed to the lord. To them Rahmatabad was a veritable Promised Land. The name of the village, "Merciville," was very appropriate. If they had any trouble or problems, such discords arose from amongst themselves.

The group that chose to live in Guledag was not as blessed. There were some tensions between the settlers and some locals. There were raids, and even a murder. Eventually, one by one, all the families moved to Rahmatabad.

Meanwhile my family decided to move once again, this time to a safer place. They abandoned Bojnurd and settled in another city, Mashhad, some 147 miles east of Bojnurd. Mashhad is "famous and revered for housing the tomb of Imam Reza, the eighth Imam of Shia."(WP) Millions of pilgrims travel to the shrine every year. It is the second most important city in Persia after Tehran, the capital of the country.

In Mashhad, my parents resumed their previous work as teamsters. My oldest sister, Margarita, found an office job with a group of young Russians, who were involved in anticommunist underground activities. She fell in love with one young man and married him against my parents' wishes. This situation posed a serious problem—a concern about the rest of the children.

Adding to this predicament, pressure from the Volkov tribe in Rahmatabad compelled my parents to abandon their independent city life and join the rest of the family. Once again, they packed their belongings and traveled the long distance westward to Rahmatabad, leaving two of the sisters, Margarita and Anna, behind.

✲   ✲   ✲

At the start, the refugees moved into crude village huts. The huts had open space in the rooftops, serving as chimneys, for cooking on an open fire. In no time, the Russian families built Russian-style houses with proper chimneys, glass windows, and whitewashed walls. The roofs were covered with sedge, later on, with homemade oak shingles.

The Persian huts were scattered throughout the village in no particular order. So, the Russians created one straight street that went through the village. On each side of the street, they erected their Russian-style houses. They designated land on the back of each house for vegetable gardens. Those who had foresight, having brought seeds from Russia, sparingly shared with their shortsighted neighbors and relatives.

There were no vacant huts when my family moved to Rahmatabad. However, there remained the family with the best hut who refused to move away when the Persian residents were ordered to vacate. Batya offered this family a price for their hut, and the owner accepted. We moved in.

Chapter 18

A Bit of History

When we escaped from the Communists into Persia, the country was in turmoil. The king of the Qajar Dynasty was very weak, thus unable to rule his country properly. It was feudal lords who controlled Persia. As a result, "in 1921 Reza Khan, Prime Minister of Iran (known as Persia at that time) and former general of the Persian Cossack Brigade, overthrew the Qajar Dynasty and became Shah."(WP)

He launched an ambitious reconstruction of the backward country newly usurped. He ordered the narrow, crooked streets of the cities be replaced with straight, wide avenues and boulevards. If some religious buildings were in the way, he had them razed. He ordered the villagers to demolish their crude huts and in their place erect brick homes.

For this purpose, he imported engineers, mainly from Germany, to build highways and railroads, and to drill tunnels in order to expedite his travels. For manual labor, he periodically compelled his citizens to work on various constructions without pay. This form of forced labor was called *bigori*. Once a year, the Shah, himself, traveled throughout his realm to see that his orders were fulfilled.

Among other reforms, the Shah also banned the wearing of the veil, called chador. The police had power to pull the veils from women in public places. People said that one of the reasons for this law was that an assassin dressed in a veil killed some official.

Reza Shah was a very decisive ruler with a strong personality, a veritable autocrat. His word was law. He ruled with cruelty, and dispensed justice on the spot. Yet he made education mandatory, including women. Woe to a parent who regularly kept his children from school! One time, a school custodian was sent to fetch a defiant father and bring him before the principal. Students were lined outside to witness lessons on "obedience." The humiliated father was ordered to take off his footwear and lie on his back with his bare feet stretched in the air. Then, the custodian applied the corporal punishment with mulberry switches on his bare feet.

The Shah was so ambitious with his *perestroika* (reconstruction in Russian); it probably cost him his demise. He was, however, able to liberate Persia from foreign occupation—for a short while. "In 1941 he [the Shah] was forced to abdicate in favor of his son, Mohammad Reza Pahlavi... Iran came under British and Russian occupation following the Anglo-Soviet invasion, which established the Persian Corridor, and would last until 1946."(WP)

Ironically, it was in this unsettled country where we found blessed refuge.

Chapter 19

Rahmatabad

Rahmatabad is situated at the base of the Elburz Mountain Range. It is located some 30 miles south of the Soviet border, which is 150 miles southeast of Ashkhabad. Sixty miles east of the Caspian Sea, and about a couple of miles south of the graveled Shah's highway lies a junction. At this junction is a village named Fazelabad, and a dirt road from this point leads to the village of Rahmatabad.

News spread throughout Persia, and even beyond its borders, about a Molokan settlement in Rahmatabad. Refugees of the same faith who had escaped from the Union Soviet Socialist Republic (USSR) decided to join us. In fact, several families immigrated to Persia from Iraq and Syria. Some of them decided to settle in Fazelabad. Soon, half of Fazelabad was populated by the Russians.

North of Rahmatabad and beyond the Shah's highway, stretch plains all the way to the Turkmenistan border. Part of Turkmenistan extends into Persia, where Turkmen tribes live in yurts. Along the western side of Rahmatabad runs a shallow gorge from the mountain pass into the plains toward Turkmenistan.

Occasionally, during spring thaw, torrents of muddy water rage through the Gorge, tumbling and tossing tree roots, logs, and boulders. When that happens, it raises thunderous, earthshaking roar that draws people to the banks of the Gorge to stare at the thrilling spectacle.

One time a shepherd with a flock of sheep was caught in such a flood. The sheep were on a rise, like an island, with water rising fast. The shepherd grabbed a lamb, put it on his shoulders, and waded across a stream. The sheep, one by one, plunged into the water, and safely climbed out of danger.

Woe to those who were caught on the other side of the Gorge. They had to hike along this ravine, downhill, through almost impassible terrain until reaching the Shah's highway and crossing the bridge to the other side.

This Gorge had a strange mystery about it. In it grew various types of vegetation unlike anything that grew around us on plains or in the forest. During the flood, water brought various seeds from distant places: grass, shrubbery, and even trees that never matured due to occasional floods. These floods changed the shape of the Gorge each flooding.

In the summertime, it is possible to cross the Gorge either on foot or by wagon. We used to cross on wagons to fetch firewood or lumber for construction.

On one side of the Gorge extends an arm from the Elburz Mountain Range all the way to the ridge of this ravine. One peak of this arm is bare so we called it "The Bald Mountain." Young people loved to climb this mountain. Once you reach the crest of it and normalize your breathing, you can see before you a spectacular view; a panorama that resembles a Persian rug. At the foot of Bald Mountain meanders the Gorge. Rahmatabad lies along the Gorge. The dirt road of this particular village is lined with mulberries and willows.

Along this road, our house is the last one on the south end of the village. If you are on top of Bald Mountain looking to your left, north, you will see Fazelabad on the Shah's highway.

At this point of the Range, the mountains are not very high. They are climbable by an average adult wearing boots. There are no rocky cliffs. The terrain is soft, covered with brush at lower altitude. A bit higher, trees grow: alder, ash, beech, elm—and at still higher elevation—linden and maple. The oak with its huge acorns is everywhere. This was my favorite spot.

View of The Bald Mountain

In the foreground is the Rechka (Речка), "River." Next is Rahma-tabad with vegetable fields. Background features part of the Elburz Mountains and distant Persian villages.

Chapter 20

A Hike to a Healing Hollow

First, you have to cross the Gorge—which we simply referred to as Речка, meaning "River"—of about 300 yards across, with rocks and boulders. During summer, there is little water. If you are agile, you can cross it by hopping from rock to rock or barefoot and wade across it in shallow spots.

On the other side of the *Rechka*, you come to a field with fragrant and pungent weeds, most abundant of which is wormwood. This noxious plant, when dead and dry, produces enormous amounts of brown pollen. Should a branch hit you in the face, you will start sneezing your brains out, as if someone threw a handful of ground black pepper into your face. And if it gets into your mouth, you'll spit your mouth dry from its bitterness.

Another thing that attracts your attention is the noise of myriad insects: the zipping of bumblebees, the scratching of grasshoppers' legs, and the incessant z-z-z-z-z of tiny pale-green field cicadas. Not far away in the woods, the jarring jee-jee-jee-jee of giant dark brown tree cicadas permeates the air.

This field is a paradise for a large variety of wild birds of various sizes, colors, sounds, and smells. There are cooing tree pigeons, and doves that weave their delicate basket-like nests among the branches. There are gray crows, rooks, nightingales, and flocks of unidentified strange-looking fowl that nest in a nearby thick growth of brush. Most of these birds are migratory.

Leaving this noisy and smelly scene, you enter an entirely different world—a profusion of wild fruit trees. There are red and black plump, tart hawthorns, juicy wild plums, black and yellow figs, sour pomegranates, tiny persimmons that pucker the mouth (but sweet when they turn from yellow to black), wild pears, crab apples, and an occasional walnut tree.

Further on, you walk along a small brook that never dries. You follow the path along this brook for about a mile uphill. The atmosphere changes noticeably—it is cooler here, and the trees taller. Soon the path leads downhill, where the air becomes much cooler.

Then, unexpectedly before you, opens up a breathtaking view. The scene is captivating—fresh, lush green vegetation. Damp banks with moss, ferns of all kinds, fragrant yellow primroses, and violets adorn this hollow. There are cyclamen here, some of which clinging to the damp walls by their hair-like roots, exposing their heart-shaped red bulbs. In the middle, there is a calm, serene pool, over which jewel-like tiny dragonflies dart from twig to twig. Inside the pool play tiny fish. The water flows noiselessly. Silence is overwhelming. If you hold your breath, you can hear yourself living.

The trees in this place are even taller than in the rest of the forest. They stretch high into the sky and branch out like huge umbrellas, allowing only some shafts of sunlight to pierce this magnificent spot. It is a perfect place for meditation. This is my Healing Hollow!

As captivating as this spot is, you want to discover more of its beauty. Going upstream, you begin to hear the gentle gurgling of water cascading downslope. After following the slippery path for some hundred yards, you are rewarded with yet another spectacular sight: clear water gently gushing out the side of the mountain (the source of this brook), the temperature of which is temperate year-round. Take off your boots, pull off the socks, roll up the pants, and wade into a tingling cool stream that sends chills through your entire body and makes your heart skip a beat.

Sitting on a half-rotten log, dangling your feet in the refreshing water, you forget the home chores, bickering, and the daily monotony. This experience calms all your concerns, bringing you peace. You want to stay here forever. But, you realize that you are only a visitor here—perhaps, even, an intruder. So you put on your socks and boots, and unwillingly retrace your steps to face the reality of your own world. Having communed with nature, you return relaxed and a bit wiser. In your memory, you will carry this healing experience for a long time.

✳   ✳   ✳

Some quarter of a century later, after immigration to America, I returned to Rahmat (short for Rahmatabad)—what a disappointment!

The weed meadow, the foothill grove and most trees are no longer there. Exotic migratory birds are no more. In place of noisy insects and wild birds, there was a funereal silence. In place of the meadow, stand some houses. In place of fowl paradise—farm fields. In place of royal oaks—cotton fields. I didn't venture to visit my Healing Hollow. I didn't want to distort the picture of my favorite spot, permanently engraved in the memory of my early youth.

Chapter 21

Cheese Factory

Shortly after Russian refugees settled comfort-ably in Rahmatabad, they decided to open up a cheese factory. One young man, Fyodor Ivanovich Muravyov had studied the art of making Dutch cheese (Gouda) while he lived in the Soviet Union as a young man. He offered his services to start the business. The elders of the village announced sk-hodka (сходка), a village counsel, and deliberated over Fyodor's proposal. After long discussion, they decided to accept Fyodor's proposal. Preparations began.

Some seven miles or so north of Rahmatabad, toward the Soviet border, were remains of an ancient civilization. The site was called "Dugabron," which in translation means "two tombs." The only sign of that civilization was a huge burial mound, Kurgan (курган, in Russian) with a large field of daffodils alongside. This mound was big enough to build a couple of palaces on top of it. By the way, in the eastern part of Russia there were several such burial mounds. Soviets had excavated them and found many treasures which are now stored in the Hermitage Museum.

On one side of the mound, the villagers started digging a large room-like space for curing cheese. The chosen site for this cellar had other alternatives—finding a treasure. However, finding this bonanza was a pipe dream. The only things they exhumed from their backbreaking labor were some animal bones. I remember Batya brought home huge jaw bones with teeth, which he displayed on a shelf in our house.

This cheese-making venture turned out to be more challenging than the villagers had imagined. To make cheese, one needs to have milk. And to make enough cheese to sell and make a profit, one needs a lot of it. The villagers, with the Muravyov brothers, scrounged and borrowed money from some non-villagers' friends. They purchased cows from Turkmen who lived at the Persian-Soviet border.

Those cows gave milk only when they had calves. After all, the cows were used to grazing on the vast plains of Turkmenia and were familiar with the Turkmen tribes and their culture. Besides, they were not very pleased to be separated from their calves, driven into Russian barns, and handled by strangers. So, these bovines went on a strike. They refused to obey these strange-smelling two-legged creatures whose language they didn't understand. If you know anything about cows, you realize that these mammas can withhold their milk. Even getting these wild cows into the barns was a struggle.

We received one of the wildest, most recalcitrant creatures of the herd. It was an early and wet spring day when Batya, and my brothers Aleksey and Mikhail (Mishka), tried to get her just near the entrance of the barn. The cow charged at them, then spun around and galloped away. Fearless teenaged Mishka grabbed her by the tail to stop her. But this wild mamma raced down the village street, dragging Mishka behind like a water skier (Mishka had moccasins on). Seeing this strange sight, village dogs joined in the chase, barking. Bystanders doubled over with laughter. Somehow from somewhere, daring young men came to Mishka's rescue and stopped the show. They lassoed this beast by the horns and brought her back.

Batya swore he would never again deal with this idiotka, his favorite swear word. But Aleksey's wife, Nastya, a brave woman, found a solution to this problem. She put on her husband's coat, one he wore when he spent some time working in Turkmenia. It was permeated with nomadic odors.

She wrapped her head with rags resembling a turban-like headdress donned by Turkish women, and then started singing like one. She slowly inched toward the idiotka and stood in front of her.

The cow looked askance at this Halloween fright and emitted a strange moo, as if to say, "Huh?" The two-legged mamma approached the four-legged one and stroked her gently with her hand. Then, still stroking and singing, she squatted down and gingerly reached for the cow's muddy teats. Finally, one could hear the rhythmic spurting flow of "chocolate" milk, because of cow's muddy teats, striking the bottom of the bucket.

Though the milking was successful, no one could drink the ambrosia of this moo of a mad cow. They poured it out, over the vegetable bed.

The two mammas became bonded. Eventually, the Halloween costume became optional and Nastya's trusted friend refused to be milked by anyone else. The experience with our cow became the talk of the village, and my sister-in-law attained a respectable regard.

I don't know how the other villagers milked their cows, but they managed to squeeze enough milk out of the udders to curdle huge, red paraffin-covered Gouda cheese. One head per family was distributed, the rest they sold.

Fyodor Muravyov's Gouda was very good, but no one had the acumen for business. So, the cheese production business was short-lived. After the initial venture, the factory folded. Perhaps the cows went dry. A few years later, the cheese-curing cellar looked like a sore wound on the imposing funeral mound—all grown over with weeds.

✳   ✳   ✳

My sister-in-law, Nastya, was a quick-witted, resourceful woman with a great sense of humor.

The roof of our house was covered with sedge (we call it foxtail). It had no ceiling; in fact, no one's house had one. For lighting, we used a kerosene lamp normally attached to the wall.

One dry summer evening, our family was having supper and sat around the table. Some of us sat with our backs facing the wall, others sat across the table facing it. Among other necessary accessories on the table, stood a large brass cup made from a cannon cartridge filled with milk. My brother, Mishka, was seated opposite Nastya and the wall with our lamp.

As he bent his neck backwards to sip the last drop of tea from his glass, he saw a tongue of flame in the ceiling and yelled, "FIRE!"

Pandemonium broke out. Children screamed in panic. Adults dashed out of the house. Except

Nastya. She sat with her back toward the lamp, calmly sipping tea. As others scrambled out looking for buckets and running toward the creek behind our house, Nastya calmly grabbed the brass cup and shot the milk into the tiny flame.

The flame hissed, and milk dripped down the wall. Only vapor and a bit of smoke puffed from the charred spot. Nastya took the lamp off the wall, set it on the table, and continued drinking tea, as if nothing had happened. Adults rushed into the house with water buckets. Nastya, feigning surprise, said, "What's this bucket brigade? As if there's a fire in the house." The rest froze, flabbergasted.

Somehow, the news spread throughout the village, "Nastya put out a fire with milk!" You can only imagine the variations of jokes about her. "Your house is on fire? Call Nastya, the famous firewoman. And bring a lot of milk!" Someone, seeing a woman milking a cow (in Russia only women milk cows), would say, "Is that for Nastya?"

Nastya relished the attention. And the Volkov men became a laughing stock.

Left to center: Sisters, Anna Volkov and Margarita (Volkov) Osadtchi, with son, Oleg Osadtchi; Nastya Volkov and brother, Aleksey Volkov; Center: Matriarch Maria Sevastyanovna Volkov; Center to right: Brother, Mikhail Volkov and wife, Antonina; sister, Tatiana and husband, Fyodor (Fred) Kashirsky.

Part VI

Chapter 22

Batya's Peculiarities

We called our father *Batya*. It is a short form of *batyushka*, which also is used to refer to a priest in the Orthodox faith.

Batya was not a farmer. But he had a unique outlook on life. He used to tell his children, "Learn new things at every opportunity. Never say, 'I will not need it. I'll never be a teacher.' You never know, but some day in the future it will come in handy."

He used to serve in the Tsarist military service. One time, a sergeant entered his barrack seeking a volunteer to whitewash a room in a newly constructed barrack. Batya volunteered without ever experiencing with such a job. He loved adventure. Whitewashing turned out to be more than dipping a brush into paint and smearing it on the wall, there was more to it. A lot more, Batya discovered.

The sergeant led him to the room, and pointing out a bucket for water, a wooden barrel, some brushes, and a pile of baked rocks. Thinking that Batya knew what to do, he said, "Here's all you need. Good luck." And he walked away.

Batya looked at all the things on the floor, but didn't see any paint. He ran after the sergeant and asked, "Where is the paint?"

The sergeant looked at Batya and said, "I thought you knew how to do all this."

"I thought I did too, but how do I paint without paint?" Batya replied in confusion.

"It's simple," explained the superior, "you place the rocks into the barrel, pour water on them, and you'll have paint," and departed.

"If you say so," Batya mumbled to himself.

He picked up the rocks. Surprise! They were as light as cork—certain types of rocks, after they're baked, become very light. He filled the barrel with rocks and poured water over them. Another surprise! The rocks began to hiss and fuss, then dissolve, then boil and shoot all over the room.

Batya ran out of the house, found the sergeant and inquired, "Come over and see what's happening." The sergeant walked inside the room. By then all the "fireworks" had exhausted their energy. Sergeant was horrified. The rocks that turned into liquid lye had run out of the barrel on the floor and splashed all over the walls.

In an angry voice the sergeant shouted, "I thought you knew how to do this. Why did you volunteer if you had no idea how to work with the lye?"

"I volunteered to whitewash, not to make paint," Batya responded.

"Why didn't you ask?"

"I was afraid you wouldn't allow me to paint."

"You learned. Now clean up the mess and continue the job." Then he burst out laughing.

Batya was very inquisitive. He always wanted to learn new things. Now that he had discovered the mysteries of rock lye, he wanted to know what type of rocks turn into lye. So, he cornered the sergeant and bombarded him with questions about what type of rocks would turn into lye. He stored the information in his head for possible future use.

Since he and farming were not compatible, he turned to his memory and information storehouse for ideas on what else besides farming he could do.

One summer day in Persia, he and Mama were crossing the Gorge. At that time, it was mostly dry. To his delight, Batya noticed that the bottom of the Gorge was covered with all types of rocks and boulders of all types of shapes and sizes. Suddenly, he shouted, "I got it! I got it!"

"What did you get?" Mama queried.

"The rocks! The rocks! That's what!"

"What 'rocks'? In your head?"

"We're going to make lye!"

"How are you going to do that?"

"You'll see."

He recruited Mama, Aleksey, and Mikhail and put them to work. They picked a spot on the riverbank and dug a huge vertical hole close to the edge of the bank. Next, at the bottom of the hole, they dug a horizontal, tunnel-like shaft and placed a grill inside the hole.

The family was drafted to carry white rocks from the Gorge to fill up the vertical hole. Batya then commandeered his crew to collect kindling and wood, and piled it under the grill, then lit a fire.

I don't know how long he baked the rocks but, with experimentation, most of the rocks did turn into what he wanted—lye.

*　　*　　*

When the villagers built themselves Russian-style houses, due to lack of other materials, they had to cover walls with clay. These walls looked drab. And so Batya, together with business-minded Mama, decided to sell lye, and supplement the family farming income.

He first painted the outside of his own house with white lye. Unsatisfied with the brightness of hue, he figured that if a bluing made the dull white fabric bright, why won't it work for the lye? With trial and error, he acquired the desired effect. The liquid lye turned slightly blue, and when he applied this concoction to a dirt wall, of course, the walls turned bluish too, but when the paint dried, it really did turn brighter white. Satisfied with the results, he spread the word among the villagers to come and look at our house. Villagers liked what they saw.

Since Mama already had some experience in the "bartering business," Batya appointed her to sales. She mostly bartered lye for goods. Soon, the whole of Rahmatabad acquired a bright new look and everybody was happy—until it rained.

Every time it rained, parts of the houses— which would soak from collected water—turned blue. Consequently, most houses showed blue streaks. Some residents complained to Batya about the ugly streaks.

He humored them by saying that they should enjoy nature's artwork, that their multicolored houses were pretty without their effort, and it didn't cost them a thing. He assured them, that when the sun appeared and weather turned dry, the houses would resume their normal color. The hut owners put up with this temporary anomaly.

Chapter 23

Mama's Education

For centuries, women have been given a bum rap. They were considered second class. However, in some isolated cultures the ruling power heavily lies primarily in the hands of women. For example, in Pakistan, where half the country is run by the seemingly anti-female Taliban, there lives a small minority group where women have more rights than their counterparts in the West.

By the way, these Kalash people say they are descendants of Alexander the Great. In Kalash culture, women choose their partners and, if the men don't keep them happy, they can discard their male partners with no repercussions for a new man. Polyandry, the practice of one wife having multiple husbands, can be found in Northern India, Nepal, Bhutan, China and Africa.

The preference of men over women, and inequality, still exists to this day even in the United States of America. Women have received less pay for the same work men do. Such inequality existed in our family. For example, my mother wanted to be literate even when she was young. When she asked her father for permission to go to school, his answer was a definite NO. "Why do you want to become literate, so you could write love letters to soldiers?" he would say.

Despite such harsh denial, Mama did learn to read in her later years when she was already married and had children. Her teacher was her husband, Batya. Mama pestered him incessantly to teach her reading. Finally, Batya capitulated.

This is what Mama told us. She had no problem with the alphabet, but she couldn't grasp the punctuation marks. Batya explained to her, "The dot with a tail is called 'comma.' It stands for 'take a breath.' The dot without a tail is called 'period.' It stands for *Zahre mor,* which in Persian it means viper venom, in other words "shut up."

Batya never taught her how to write in cursive. Mama managed to read words only in print. With this less than rudimentary education, she read her Bible school lessons daily and the whole Bible at least once.

✶   ✶   ✶

Batya inherited a gift of healing from his mother. He was the "doctor" in the family. For example, he had contracted trachoma, a highly communicable eye disease, but he was able to prevent it from spreading to other members of the family. He had his own private towels, and instructed Mama to boil them in water to keep others from using them. He always had an ample supply of medications for various ailments. He also had a habit of tasting the potency of all medicines so he could dispense the right amount of medicine according to the age of the patient.

Mama made it a point to learn this art of healing. She did learn some of it, and practiced her limited ability on every person who needed help without charging anything for her services. Eventually, her fame spread around the neighboring villages. Locals called her *Duktur Maryam*, "Doctor Mary."

Quite often Persian mothers brought their infants to our house for treatment with various physical ailments: eye or skin infection, dysentery, dislocation, and many other ailments. She also treated urinary retention. She became interested in this malady because two of her sons died in infancy from an inability to urinate.

One time, the head of the neighboring village, Aliabad, developed urinary retention, so he called Mama for help. She cured him of his problem with bluing. How she came by this method of treating urinary problems is still a mystery. For her services, the village head rewarded her with a lamb, a typical practice of gratitude.

Mama was not squeamish. She had a unique method of getting foreign objects from the eyes. When she couldn't get something from the eye the conventional way, she would use her tongue. As you know, the tongue is the most sensitive part of human anatomy. With it, she could feel even the smallest foreign object in the eye and she would lick it out.

Stomach disorders, she treated with a liquid medicine called *"kinderbalsam."* She purchased this medicine in an apothecary, a drug store and would treat small children with it. It tasted like licorice. A few drops of it in mild tea tasted good. Children liked it.

When we lived in Iran in the 1930s and 1940s, most medicine was made on the premises in apothecaries. Before we emigrated to America in December of 1950, Mama went to her favorite pharmacist and asked him to write her a recipe for kinder balsam. He wrote it in Latin, since Latin was the language of medicine in Iran. Mama cherished that recipe like a treasure.

In America, when her supply of this elixir was diminishing she went to the drugstore with her recipe, but alas, she could not find a druggist who could read Latin. She was not one to give up. She went from one drugstore to another until she found a pharmacy on Boyle Street in Los Angeles.

An old Jewish pharmacist was delighted to see such a relic of the days gone by. He concocted Mama's panacea and translated the recipe into English—and he didn't even charge her for his efforts. He considered it a pleasure to mix the ingredients from this antiquated recipe.

When Mama died in 1967, we used up the leftovers of her medicine on our children. As for her recipe, no one knows what happened to it.

Chapter 24

"The Shah Is Coming!"

Shortly after his coronation to the Persian throne in 1926, Reza Shah Pahlavi launched his modernization and reconstruction plans for his realm. One phase of this reconstruction was dedicated to improving infrastructure. Buildings had to meet then-new safety standards.

Highways were widened and made straight, railroads extended, tunnels drilled, bridges constructed, so on and so forth. To ensure that his mandates were carried out properly, the new Shah personally made annual inspection tours of his empire in black German-made sedans. In major cities, he had royal palaces constructed where he could stop with his entourage during his inspections. He maintained a very strict traveling schedule.

To show Padeshah that his demands were being met, government officials had citizens build and maintain highways, especially for the days of his visit. They would also build brick houses along the roads and streets of his itinerary.

For labor force of the king's projects, local governors forced all able-bodied men to dedicate one day a month to free labor. Each laborer rendered his duty according to his profession or ability—clerks, carpenters, bricklayers, et cetera.

The Russian villagers would bring their wagons to haul whatever was required. This form of forced labor was called *bigori*. Even then, locals were able to skirt around the orders of their demanding autocrat. They built the prescribed brick houses along the streets and roads through which the Shah would pass, and painted each house a different color—only on the sides that faced the royal highway. On the day of his visit, all residents were ordered to hide their rubbish, out of sight, behind their freshly painted houses. As soon as Padeshah disappeared, areas would resume their former appearance.

On one such occasion, the village school principal ordered parents to buy expensive uniforms for their schoolchildren to wear on such eventful occasions. For the day of this royal appearance, students had to memorize the National Anthem. They were to wash themselves, keep fingernails neat, and maintain trim and combed hair.

Before morning inspection of the students, the principal lined up the best-looking and best-dressed students in the front row along the royal highway. He also positioned his bright students front and center, just in case the king would deign to stop and ask them questions. Usually, the royal caravan would zoom through without even slowing down, leaving the meticulously dressed students in the dust.

One time, the Russian "delegation," all decked out in their best peasant apparel, decided to welcome his majesty. By the side of the highway, they set up a table with white linen tablecloth, a samovar with proper teapot on top, teacups, sugar, and baked goodies.

As soon as the Russians heard the sound of the motorcade, the men stood at attention. The royal caravan slowed down and came to a stop, motors still running. The Russian men took off their hats and bowed low. The King exited his vehicle and approached the delegation. He greeted them in Russian.

He recognized them as Russians; after all, some time ago, he had served as an officer in the Persian Cossack regiment, commanded by a Russian commander, Colonel Staroselsky. Padeshah asked them a few questions, then turned around with his retinue. They boarded their sedans and took off, leaving the honored Russians in a cloud of dust.

Chapter 25

Mama and the Sheriff

According to Persian law, each village had a head, called *katkhudo*, who kept order among the residents. The villagers of Rahmatabad voted in a man, named Vasiliy, who had an ambitious, domineering personality with some questionable ethics, hidden selfishness, and vengeance.

One day Vasiliy, the *katkhudo*, approached my father and said that since he was the head of the village, he was entitled to live in a better house. He suggested to Batya that they exchange their houses. Batya demanded to see such a law in writing. Of course, no such thing existed.

This happened before the villagers decided to build a straight road through the village. Vasiliy drew a map so that our hut would be in the way. When Batya was asked to tear down our house, he said, "Over my dead body." A feud was born.

A time came when the Persian government demanded that these Russian refugees do some *bigori*, free labor for the government. And since Vasiliy was the head of our village, it was his duty to schedule villagers to perform this obligation.

Because we were Sabbath keepers, we did not work from sundown Friday to sundown Saturday. So, Vasiliy scheduled our adult men to do *bigori* on their holy Sabbath.

Mama was a fearless, decisive woman. On several occasions, I saw her grab a snake by the tail, shake it, throw it, and then smash its head with her heel. She never hesitated to dispense justice on the spot, as she saw fit.

On one occasion during a city visit, Mama and I were walking along the sidewalk, and an urchin squirted gutter water from his bamboo water gun, into my face. I cried. A police officer laughed.

Mama approached the cop and said, "Your job is to prevent such hooliganism and not to laugh at it," and slapped him in the face. Mama knew the Moslem law about women. Women were inviolable. No man was ever to touch a woman—not even an official. A woman is property of a man!

I was a curious kid and enjoyed eavesdropping on adults. One day I heard my parents having a serious conversation. I heard Mama saying, "Why are you so sad today?"

"It's Vasiliy again," Batya confided. "He scheduled us to do bigori on Sabbath."

"How dare he!" Mama responded in a threatening voice.

"He is angry and wants revenge," Batya explained. "I told him that Saturday is our holy Sabbath, and that nothing in the world could make me violate God's holy day. He only said, 'We'll see.'"

"The swine," Mama uttered.

"Next Saturday," Batya continued, "he threatened to bring the sheriff over, to force us go to work on our Sabbath. If I refuse, I will be arrested."

When I heard the word "arrest," I felt like crying.

"Just let him try it!" Mama was militant.

Saturday morning came. I was still in bed but not sleeping. Mama was outside, by the brick oven that Batya had constructed for her, tending to breakfast and Sabbath dinner. Batya was having his private Sabbath morning worship.

Suddenly I heard some strange voices outside. I was all ears.

"Salaam-alaikum," greeted the sheriff curtly, addressing Mama.

"Alaikum-salaam. What do you want?" Mama didn't sound friendly.

"Where's your husband?" demanded the sheriff.

"He's in the house saying Sabbath prayers."

"Tell him to come out," he ordered.

"One moment," mumbled Mama, and shuffled into the hut.

Vasiliy grinned. For some reason, I did not like that grin.

Mama entered the hut and whispered, "They're outside."

Batya hung his towel on the beam, ready to face the unwanted "guests."

Mama came out of the house and said, "He'll be here when he's finished with his prayers."

I heard an angry grunt coming from outside. In Persia, in an autocratic government, nobody makes officials wait, and an alien doing that was definitely asking for trouble.

As soon as Batya left the house, I jumped out of bed, picked up our dog, Jangal, a small white mutt with brown spots. I put him on my lap, sat quietly by the door, and peeked through a crack.

I saw the sheriff, with a black mustache, sitting atop a horse. Next to him, leaning on his hoe, stood Vasiliy. Vasiliy had a gaunt, bony face and a long grayish beard that looked like a horse's tail. Both men looked angry.

Mama stood by the brick oven with a poker. She wore a plain dress with apron, and a triangular babushka on her head.

Mama was as gentle as an angel, but when any of her family members were threatened, she turned into a mama tiger. On this Sabbath morning, she did not look holy.

Batya came out slowly and calmly approached the angry men.

"*Salaam alaikum,*" he greeted the sheriff with a calm voice. Then turning to Vasiliy, he greeted him "good morning" in Russian, in the same courteous voice. "*Dobroye ootro.* What can I do for you, men?"

I don't think the men liked the way Batya greeted them, because the sheriff groaned angrily, and without returning the required response to a greeting, he gripped his bullwhip. He barked, "Why aren't you at work like you were ordered?"

When I saw the whip, I began to shiver, and squeezed Jangal tightly.

"I told the honorable *katkhudo* I could not work on my Sabbath," explained Batya calmly." I would be glad to work on Sunday—tomorrow."

"Sunday's quota is full. We need you today," cut in Vasiliy.

"Many Sunday-keeping men would be glad to trade days with me," added Batya calmly.

"Don't argue with government officials!" snapped the sheriff. "Hitch your horses right now and go! You're already late!"

"I have already explained to you," said Batya in the same calm tone. "I cannot work on my Sabbath." Then he turned around to go into the hut.

The sheriff was beside himself. He swung his whip like lightning and whomped Batya so hard that the whip wound around Batya's waist. I screamed.

Mama grabbed her poker and whacked the sheriff on the back. She then swung it around and struck the horse on the rump. The poor nag reared on her hind legs and galloped toward our vegetable garden as if she were on a racetrack. The sheriff almost lost his balance. He let go of the reins, dropped his whip, and gripped the saddle to prevent from toppling over.

Jangal slipped out of my arms like a wet bar of soap and dashed, barking after the sheriff. The mare jumped over the pomegranate fence and kept on galloping through the cucumbers, tomatoes, eggplants, and squashes.

Vasiliy froze on the spot like Lot's wife. Then Mama turned on him. He suddenly came to life and dashed away as if attacked by a swarm of hornets. He dropped his hoe and kept on running.

Mama picked up the sheriff's whip and the hoe and flung them after Vasiliy with some expletives. Then she shouted, "Don't you ever set your foot on our property again! I swear I'll kill you!" And she spat on the ground.

I expected soldiers to come any minute and shoot all of us, including Jangal. Mama came over, hugged me, and said gently, "Don't worry, son. Everything's all right. No one's going to hurt us. Trust me." She stroked my head, wiped my face with her apron, and gave me a kiss.

I couldn't figure it out. How could Mama be an angel one moment and a tiger the next?

From that day on, we were never bothered by Vasiliy and the sheriff, and Batya was never again scheduled to do *bigori* on Saturdays.

Chapter 26

Batya's Final Trek

Batya did not live in Rahmatabad very long. In 1936, five years after we crossed the border, he became ill with pneumonia. He was 48. I was only six.

Mama and my brother, Mikhail, took him to the city that night in a wagon, some 30 miles away. They took me along with them. It was a stormy night with rain and violent wind.

Finally, we got to the hospital. It was closed for the night. We trekked to the doctor's house. We knocked on his door, no one answered.

Since we had no other alternative, we went to a caravanserai. We lodged there, on the mezzanine floor. It was a large, shared space with several large stalls without doors, in which there was just enough room for families to lodge, with separation but no privacy.

In the morning I heard Mom calling, "Isay! Isay!" No answer. She called louder. Then she looked under the blanket. After a pause, she whispered to Mikhail, "Father died." That was all she said.

Mama and Mikhail had to go to the market to buy things for the funeral. They hitched the horses to the wagon and drove off, leaving me alone with my dead father. After what seemed to me a long time, I felt I was abandoned for good. I started crying.

Suddenly, I was startled, when I heard a powerful though gentle voice say, "Why are you crying?"

"My mother and brother went shopping and I am afraid," I sobbed through tears.

I didn't dare tell the patrolling gendarme, a form of police, that I was guarding my dead father's body.

I was afraid there might be some trouble. Even at the age of six, I was aware of superstitions about dead people on the premises. The gendarme assured me that everything would be fine and that they would return soon. I was so glad when he left without asking any more questions.

Was I happy when Mama and Mikhail returned!

Without attracting any attention unto ourselves, we were afraid, even, to show our grief.

In total silence, Mikhail and Mama carried Batya and gently laid him on our wagon, and covered him with a blanket. The horses were still hitched to the wagon from the visit to town. Then, Mama and I loaded our things on the wagon, while Mikhail paid the caravanserai owner.

Finally, we slowly trekked back to Rahmatabad.

*   *   *

When we arrived back home, I noticed the devastation the storm had caused. Tree branches scattered all around, toppled trees, houses without rooftops. This havoc made me shudder. Then, I noticed that the brick oven my father had constructed for my mother had collapsed during the storm. When I saw a pile of muddy bricks where the oven had stood, a thought crossed my mind. The oven symbolized my father. The bread maker and bread baker were gone. I did not say anything to anyone.

I was overcome with painful confusion.

Behind our house, there was an abandoned rice mill that the Shubin family had turned into a wheat mill. Next to this, the villagers chose a section of land for a cemetery.

My Grandfather Stepan Volkov was one of the first to be buried there. His was the only grave that had a tombstone which identified his name and dates of his birth and death. This homemade headstone was chiseled by Batya.

Batya's final resting place is next to his father.

Chapter 27

Mama and the Shah of Persia

Padeshah would make periodic inspections of his empire during spring, when nature adorned itself for the occasion. Perhaps, the Monarch chose this time when nature looked her best. During his travels, the King would need some respite.

About 30 miles from our village, stood one of his palaces, in the city of Gorgan (formerly Asterabad, in honor of the Biblical Queen Esther). Just before the Shah's arrival, the palace was cleaned, dusted and polished. The grounds were adorned with exotic, fragrant bushes, trees, and blooms that charmed the eye and tickled the olfactory senses.

To bring the palace to a festive state, city officials hired horticulturists for the grounds. For palace cleaning, they hired local women. The latter did not please the supervisors.

Then someone suggested trying the Russian women. These women did their best to please the officials. The supervisors liked what they saw. From then on, every year it was the Russian women who were given the honor to clean this royal palace. To them it was such an honor and an adventure, they would do it without pay just for the privilege.

Now, when these peasant women saw the electric lights, they were fascinated. The young women, especially, had great fun playing with the two-way light switches. One would stand by one wall switch, flicking, the other flicking at the other end, playing with switches like little children. These female laborers were paid upon completion of a satisfactory job.

Occasionally, my mother also volunteered to help clean the palace to earn some extra money. These women worked very hard, so the inspectors could find no pretense to minimize their wages or refuse payment.

On one day, the Shah surprised officials by arriving a day earlier. To get the cleaning crew out of sight of the King, officials loaded the women on trucks and took them to the edge of the city on the King's Highway, where they could hitchhike home. They were told to report back later for their earnings.

Seeing the deceitfulness of the inspectors, Mama decided that this turn of events did not suit her. She said, "Women, you'll never see your hard-earned money."

"What do you suggest, Maria?" someone asked.

"We'll march right back to the palace and demand to see the Shah," she said with resolution.

"Are you out of your mind to do such a thing?"

"Just wait and see. We'll get what's coming to us," Mama assured them.

"Yes, we'll get what's coming to us—sticks," said one sharp-tongued woman, sarcastically.

"I don't know what you will do. I'm going after my money." She picked up her belongings and started walking with determination. If there was one thing Mama hated more than anything else in the world—it was injustice.

One by one, the female brigade followed.

As the women approached the palace, the guards stopped the procession, raising their rifles.

"What do you want?" demanded one guard.

"We have an appointment with the Shah," Mama announced purposefully, as if she really had that engagement. Then she turned to her delegation and said, "Act bravely."

To cross the Shah was to jeopardize one's life. The guards were taken aback. They were in a quandary. Let the women through? Or send them back? Either way, they faced consequences. Had there been one or two of them, the solution would have been simpler, but there was a whole detachment of them. The guards let the detail through.

The women entered the palace square, and Mama announced loudly, "We demand to see the Shah."

The officials became confused and embarrassed. They didn't know how the Shah would react to this theatrical sight. Somehow, from somewhere, Padeshah appeared on the scene.

At that instant, the women fell on their knees and lowered their heads to the ground.

The Shah asked one of his attendants to inquire what these women wanted.

Mama, still kneeling, addressed the Shah in Russian, "Your majesty, we have cleaned your palace for your arrival, but we have not been paid for our work. We were just driven out of the city on a truck. We want to be paid."

The Shah was taken aback with such a brash woman. Turning to his officials, he commanded angrily, "Pay these women right now and let them go in peace!" Then, he turned around and briskly walked away.

The women were paid. They too turned around and walked their merry way rejoicing. Mama became the talk of the village for some time. Her respect in society was confirmed instantly. They probably thought, *Don't mess with this woman.*

Reza Shah Pahlavi.

Royal palace grounds, Gorgon.

Chapter 28

Unequally Yoked

You shall not plow with an ox and a donkey yoked together.
Deuteronomy 22:10, NIV

Early spring was time for plowing and sowing. The weather was still wintery. Sleep, on a down mattress and a down pillow, under a down comforter, was deliciously wonderful. Until I heard, "Wake up, Yasha. It's the third time I'm calling you. It's time to plow the new field."

It finally reached my thinking center, and I unwillingly slithered out from under heavenly warmth and into the cruel chilly world.

"Plow the new field?" I asked in a groggy voice.

It was just mama and I.

"How are we going to do that? Pull the plow ourselves?"

"We have a horse, and we borrowed Grishka (a camel) from the Bakholdins. You sit on the camel, animals pull, and I walk behind the plow. Simple," explained Mama.

A horse and a camel, a woman and a child.

"Mama, why do you come up with such things?" I insisted, "What will people say? They're already making fun of us."

"If we listen to what people say, we might as well stop living," replied Mama. She was known for doing things differently.

I knew well that once Mama made up her mind, nothing could change it. I had to try just in case. Besides, for a thirteen-year-old boy to abandon his "royal" bed on a cold predawn morning was criminal. I pressed, "But it's against the Bible. Besides, I'm scared of camels. They're mean and they spit."

"If you don't hurt the camel, it won't hurt you. I don't think God wants us to starve."

I knew I could not out-argue Mama. I yielded.

I hated farming to begin with. I'd rather read than plow. But it was already March, a perfect time to sow barley and wheat for August harvest, and we couldn't delay it any longer.

After a hurried breakfast, Mama and I managed to haul the plow onto the wagon, and hitch Grishka to it. I held the reins, while Mama rode Serukha, our white mare, behind the wagon, we headed toward the new field.

This field hadn't been plowed in ages, and it was overgrown with artichoke-like thistles, camels' favorite food. We dragged the plow off the wagon and hitched the animals to it. Grishka didn't mind the thistles, but our mare was getting very jittery.

Before starting a new project, according to our custom, Mama asked me to offer a prayer, which included a recitation of the Lord's Prayer.

After the "Amen," Mama boosted me on top of the nervous mare. Serukha had never been yoked with this kind of beast of burden. In addition, the two animals weren't the best of friends either. From the mare's back, I scrambled to the top of Grishka. I felt comfortable sitting on the soft hump of the camel. Grishka paid no attention to all the fuss. He was too busy stuffing his cavernous stomach with his favorite dessert.

We were ready to cut the first furrow. I was perched on top of the camel, way above the horse; Mama was behind the plow.

"No-o-oh," I ordered—that's "giddy-up" in Russian horse language—and pulled on Grishka's reins. Serukha lunged forward, but Grishka didn't budge. He didn't understand the horse language. He just stood there, paying no attention to this thing on top of his hump. I struck him on his side with a switch. The beast growled and started taking long strides. The mare kept prancing after him. I began swaying back and forth, as if churning butter.

Grishka didn't follow the straight line as I tried to guide him; he lunged after the best thistles. This made the furrow behind Mama look like a giant black sidewinder rattlesnake.

Wanting to show the stubborn beast who was in charge, I lashed Grishka on the head with the switch. Grishka stopped on the spot, took a deep breath, and turned his head around like a cobra. I heard a gurgling sound in Grishka's throat, like a sewer pipe about to explode. I knew exactly what was coming. I tried to duck. Too late. Grishka doused me with foamy pre-digested breakfast. The smelly, slimy puke made me sick to my stomach. I lashed the brute on the head again. This time he wanted to let me know who's in charge: he took off as if he were in a race.

Serukha started bucking and tried to keep up with her partner. Mama lost the plow, and with her bonnet flying around her head, kept shouting, "Stop! Pull on the reins!" I was too petrified to do anything. The clanging plow behind me made me cling to the camel like a tick.

The plow snagged a rock, somersaulted in the air, and banged against the ground. The wheels came off and rolled in opposite directions. I yelled in terror, "Mama-a-ah! Help!"

I tried to stop Grishka by pulling on the reins with all my mini-might, but when he lunged for another thistle, I let go of the reins so I wouldn't be pulled off my perch and be chopped to bits with the pieces of the plow. The plow broke loose from the animals. Serukha yanked on her reins, bucked away from Grishka, and galloped in the opposite direction. The camel hopped toward the tallest growth of thistles, with helpless and terrified me clinging to his back. Grishka stopped in the middle of the thistle field and proceeded refilling his stomach.

The camel's salty, sweaty back made me itch, and I became sicker and madder—but still helpless. I looked around and asked, "How am I going to get out of this mess?"

Then I saw Mama galloping toward me astride Serukha with her hair waving in the air. She approached the thistle field and urged the unwilling mare into the field.

"Are you OK, son?" she shouted.

Seeing rescue at hand, I suddenly became brave, and yelled back, "I'm just fine, Mama."

"Thank God," she said with relief. Still astride Serukha, she grabbed Grishka's reins and led him out of the prickly predicament. Then, she added sadly, "Now, let's pick up the plow pieces and head home."

Seeing Mama's disappointed face, I felt sorry for her. Somehow, I felt responsible for the ruined day. Then a thought crossed my mind about yoking animals unequally.

Yashka (author) on top of Grishka.

Maria Sevastyanovna Volkova on threshing floor with her grandchildren, Anna and Ivan.

A young Yakov guarding newly washed wheat drying on the threshing floor.

Chapter 29

More Serious Responsibilities

I always kept busy. I was a helper to some adults in the family, whatever anyone needed. As I grew up, more serious responsibilities were laid upon my shoulder. However, I should add, education took precedence over all other chores. To Mama, keeping me from school to do chores, no matter how urgent, was a cardinal sin.

Summer was the time when I was doing chores with my sister Nadya, who was a couple of years older than I was. Our adventures together would come later.

One responsibility that was solely mine was guarding a melon patch day and night. One day my brother Aleksey took some poles, branches, and straw, and loaded them onto the wagon, and the two of us headed for the melon patch outside of village. Once there, we unloaded and took everything into the center of the patch. With these items, we constructed a twelve-foot watchtower, вышка (vyshka). We even added a crude roof to provide shade.

That done, Aleksey gave me some instructions and went home, leaving me alone, saying he will check up on me in a few days. In my possession, I had a bottomless tin drum, a stick, a 20-gauge shotgun with cartridges, and some provisions. My job was to guard the melons and watermelons from thieves, and wild animals, especially porcupines, wild pigs, and occasionally black bears.

The porcupines lived underground in endless labyrinthine passages. When they entered a watermelon patch, they would crack a watermelon, bite a piece of it, eat the soft part, and spit the rind in neat piles. They did not discriminate between ripe and green watermelons; as long it was juicy, they consumed it. I'm not sure if they even had any taste buds. The pigs were nasty critters; they lived up to their name—PIGS.

Usually they roamed in packs. When they entered a patch, they bulldozed through it. They not only ate the fruit of the vine, they uprooted the vines and trampled over them. I hated them with a passion!

The bears, on the other hand, were very neat and discriminating; they would select a ripe watermelon, split it neatly and, just as neatly, scrape the red portion of the watermelon up to the rind and leave it on the ground without breaking it into pieces. I marveled at their craft of selecting the best of the crop and eating it so delicately. I hated them nevertheless. They beat me to the best watermelons.

My responsibility was to keep the crop from these marauders, including the two-legged ones. In the mornings, I would inspect to assess the damage then spend the rest of the time sitting on top of the watchtower daydreaming and napping. At night, I'd bang on the tin drum that I suspended from the "roof" and sing songs or yell expletives as loud as my throat could handle. Sometimes, I would climb down from my watch with a tin drum and a stick, and march around the patch banging on the drum, yelling, and singing Russian folk songs. Sometimes I would descend with the shotgun and just tramp through the melon field quietly.

I had many encounters on my watch. I had no fear of anything—forest or field, darkness or brightness, insect or wild beast. Not even snakes made me jump out of my skin.

One night, after a mild rain that made the field soft but not muddy, the sky was overcast, but the moon still shed some dusk light through the clouds, I decided to make a reconnaissance of my territory. With a shotgun in hands, I stepped through the soft field slowly and noiselessly, hoping to come upon a critter. Just a couple of steps ahead of me I noticed a dark shape. I stopped and listened. I heard some crunching. I surmised immediately it was a porcupine.

The beast was so engrossed in enjoying his meal that it didn't hear me approach. I had heard someone say that if you shoot at something too close, the muzzle of the rifle may explode. So, foolishly I grabbed the gun by the muzzled, raised it over my head and whacked my enemy with the stock of my gun. The Porky took off as fast as his short legs could carry him. I started chasing him, but I couldn't keep up with him. It was not until the following morning that it dawned on me what injury I could have inflicted upon myself. My belly would have been a depository of some lead pellets.

One night I had an encounter with a black bear. Along one edge of the watermelon patch, we planted several rows of sunflowers. At this time of year, sunflowers were at the prime of harvest. Once again, I decided to inspect my territory. As usual, I slid down my watch and started pacing stealthily, listening to every sound.

Soon I heard a crackling sound among the sunflowers. I didn't think it was a human sneaking into our sunflower patch enjoy sunflower seeds. I gingerly headed toward the sound. Suddenly in front of me, I saw a large black shape. Without the slightest hesitation, I pulled on the trigger.

The instant flash of the gunshot revealed a bear. In panic, I dropped the gun and flew toward safety. I don't know how I was able to scramble up my perch, trembling but I did.

In the morning, I went to fetch my weapon. I had no problem finding the spot of my encounter with the beast, because there was a path of knocked-down sunflower stocks pointing toward the watchtower, and even a larger path of flattened plants pointed the opposite direction. I was so used to banging, yelling, swearing, and singing night after night that sometimes I went through this routine in my sleep, without waking myself.

Chapter 30

My Brother Aleksey

Aleksey Isayevich was the oldest in our family. He loved animals, people, nature, and farming. However, he was not endowed with exceptional scholastic "stuff."

Even in childhood, he loved animals. He had no fear of them, followed them at every opportunity. One time he approached a horse from the rear and tried to pet it. The mare was startled and bucked him in the face, severely damaging one of his eyes, making him cross-eyed for life.

That experience did not discourage him from loving horses and caring for them. He never mistreated animals; in fact, when they didn't perform their job properly, he would inspect the reasons for their misbehavior. There were occasions when a harness would rub against the horsehide; in that case, he would take a handkerchief out of his pocket and place it under the rough spot. His wife, Nastya, always scolded him for ruining his handkerchiefs.

He never used the whip to urge them pull a loaded wagon up a hill; he would get down the wagon and push it, all along urging the horses compassionately, "Come on, darlings! Pull! Pull!" When possible, he would stop the horses and put a rock or a log under the rear wheel to prevent the wagon from rolling back, and give the animals some rest. Before saddling the horse, he would inspect the saddlecloth to make sure there was nothing rough stuck to the pad to irritate the back of the horse.

Aleksey treated all people and all races with courtesy and respect. Occasionally he would go to the northern part of Iran, where the Turks lived, a part of Turkmenistan that extended into Iran. What business he had there I never knew.

On his first visit there, one man invited Aleksey and some of his own friends to his yurt. At dinnertime, all men sat in a circle on a homemade felt rug. There was a cauldron containing some kind of stew in the middle of the circle, with a long-handled wooden spoon in the pot. As custom dictated, the host would offer the spoon first to the honored guest, in this case to Aleksey, to be passed around.

Being ignorant of this custom, Aleksey proceeded to eat the stew, while the rest of the guests sat patiently staring at the honored guest. After dipping his spoon repeatedly into the cauldron, his neighbor to the right, nudged him on the side with his elbow and whispered to pass the spoon to another guest on his right.

To his surprise and embarrassment, Aleksey noticed that the guests passed the only spoon around to the rest of the guests until it returned back to him. By then, his appetite had escaped him. Not to embarrass the host, he summoned all the courage he had and ate with the burping guests.

One time Aleksey took me along to Turkmenia, when I was still in my early teens. I don't remember a thing of that trip, except for one thing that stuck in my mind—the two wives of the man we visited. I was appalled. I imagined all kinds of bizarre scenes of what went on in bed during the night, not realizing that the two wives had separate yurts.

Since I was not much help on the farm, and because I went to school, Aleksey hired a young Turkmen named Kurd. He had a slight limp, but he was industrious and good-natured. Kurd learned his job very quickly, and anticipated Aleksey's every wish. Aleksey took a liking to him, and they became bonded. How and how much Aleksey paid him, I had no idea. Kurd became like a member of the family.

One day Kurd disappeared, and rumors spread that there was a gang of marauders headed by a young limping man. This gang stole farm animals. Everyone's fingers pointed to our Kurd.

One night all the cattle in our village disappeared. Early in the morning, our cattle returned. The villagers, putting two-and-two together, deducted that Aleksey Isayevich had had a hand in this business. They claimed that robbers picked out Aleksey's cattle and shooed them homeward. Aleksey just laughed at the gross absurdity.

Later in the day, a few more cattle returned to their stalls. Nothing of the accusation materialized. However, the seeds of suspicion germinated in the minds of the villagers. It took a while before Aleksey regained his respect in the village.

One dark night, Kurd came to our house with some of his cohorts and asked for something to eat. Aleksey asked Nastya to feed them. She complied, but grumbled the whole time and reprimanded Kurd harshly for his evil ways. She told her "guests" they were nothing but bandits. Kurd just smiled sweetly.

As the "honored bandits" ate, Aleksey lectured Kurd on his immoral profession and begged him to give it up, or they would lead to a sad end. Kurd just ate hungrily and said nothing. As soon as they finished their meal, they quietly slipped into the darkness of the night and disappeared.

Again, rumors went around. This time, apparently, Kurd's band was apprehended and punished. How they were punished, we never did find out.

As I mentioned before, Aleksey was indiscriminately friendly with everybody. Occasionally, the Turks brought wheat to local water mills to grind it into flour. Since the water mills were at the foothills of the Elburz Mountain Range, where there was water and where it was possible to build such mills, and since Rahmatabad was near the mountain range, they had to go through our village.

You see, the Turkmen lived on the steppes, and water was available through qanats only. A qanat is an ancient water system that brings underground water to the surface. Some of these qanats were constructed in ancient times, and they still function well.

The Turks would carry their loads atop caravans of camels. Sometimes they would park their camels on our threshing floor for rest. When Aleksey was not at home, they would proceed on their way. When he was home, he would meet them while they were approaching our house and invited them in for a meal.

A couple of times I asked to ride one of the dromedaries. The "guests" would humor me. My joy was indescribable. My brave sister Nadya would join me. My older sister, Tanya, wouldn't come near them. One of the Turks would put me on a resting animal's back and position Nadya behind me.

The scary fun was clinging to the saddle, as the camel would rise to his long legs. First, to its front knees—you may slide backwards off the camel's back. Second, the behemoth elevates to its rear knees—you slide forward. Third, front legs—slide backward, higher from the ground. Fourth, the hind legs—slide forward, still higher. Meanwhile, screaming Nadya would cling to me.

Finally, you feel, as if you're atop a skyscraper. When you are high in the air, above your tall Dad, you're surprised to discover that your father is balding. And when a camel starts walking, you begin to sway back and forth, like a willow in a breeze.

A humble yurt; no place for a guilty kid to stand in the corner. (WP)

A modern yurt.(WP)

Chapter 31

The Family of Aleksey Yakovlevich Volkov

As long as we live on this painful planet, we are constantly faced with a myriad of choices, some are trite, others are life changing. To obtain desired outcome requires painful sacrifices.

Utmost on the scale of needs of survival, is subsistence and security. Following those, are the freedoms of value and choice. There are always price and risks involved, and we must count the cost for our choices—what we need to sacrifice.

We constantly need to make choices, sometimes very painful ones. The Volkovs and their friends and relatives opted for freedom of religion over creature comforts. To them their walk with God was dearer than life itself.

Had my cousin Aleksey Yakovlevich Volkov abandoned his values and considered adopting Communism so that his material comfort would be supplied, life would have been different—but even that decision offered no guarantee.

By opting to keep their values, and like the rest of families in this village, they abandoned homes, land, crops, and most of their moving possessions. They lost their country and their identity. They became stateless. Not only that, they lost temporal security, free medical help, and access to their children's free education.

In choosing their own independent lifestyle, they lost all of the aforementioned values and more. Luckily, a Persian khan gave the refugees a village—even though, the huts they occupied were sooty from open fire inside the living quarters. They had to start their lives in an Islamic country, from "scratch."

This family had five children, two daughters and three boys. In the process of establishing their life in Iran, their mother died. At that time, the oldest daughter, Tatyana, had already been married against her parents' will and lived away from her community. The oldest son, Vasiliy, was 17, Yakov 14, Ivan 8, and the youngest daughter, Dunyasha, was only five. The men couldn't cope with raising a five-year-old child, so they gave her away for adoption to a childless family.

A year later, Father died. The farm was left to the care of two teenagers and an eight-year-old boy. Thanks to the relatives who came to the rescue the first difficult years. Vasiliy was responsible for the farm work, and the younger siblings took care of the housework. Being gifted farmers, the young men adapted to farming and successfully survived.

Orphaned children always carried with them a painful stigma. No "decent" parents wanted to give their daughters to guideless boys. Neither did they want their sons to marry a motherless girl who had not been instructed in the art of family management, not realizing that the best teacher in this case was life itself that taught them survival skills and self-sufficiency at an early age.

It was not until later in life, that they proved themselves. The society realized the fact that these boys survived and succeeded in life. Only then, were they respected and accepted into their society. In later years, when the members of this family immigrated to the United States, the land of opportunity, Yakov and Ivan (John) became successful vintners.

All three brothers taught themselves how to read. Vasiliy, the oldest, became avid reader of Russian classics, and the youngest, Ivan (John) was a Bible reader in his church.

Part VII

Chapter 32

Spirituality Among the Refugees

Originally, when this group of people began to study the Bible and discovered the discrepancy between the Bible and the Church traditions, they broke off from mother church.

Because the Orthodox Church, with the support of the state, treated these people as rebellious heretics, and because they suffered together, these "heretics" became solidified. For lack of formal houses of worship, the rebels' religious differences did not interfere with their struggle for survival, so they worshiped together. In time, though, among them arose new leaders that were more versed in Scripture.

At first, their followers consisted of their relatives and friends. As members increased in number, more followers joined in. Inevitably, there were groups who interpreted the Bible differently; consequently, different communities were formed.

However, in exile, when persecutions relaxed, differences in their beliefs became more pronounced.

Naturally, some aggressive and more literate individuals vied for superiority and leadership. With farsighted vision, some began to build larger houses with spacious living rooms to accommodate large gatherings of followers.

Naturally, they began to worship separately. However, they did remain amicable. During festivals, weddings, and especially during funerals, all groups celebrated or honored such events collectively.

Though there were minor differences in beliefs, the system of worship remained mostly the same. They sang and prayed the same songs—Bible passages and recitations, mainly from the Psalms. During worship, they also dressed alike, in the Russian peasant holiday attire.

The largest group consisted of Molokans, which means, "of the milk." Where and why this name originated, no one really knows for sure. And then, this group broke off into two slightly different congregations.

To this day, the larger group consists of what is known as Прыгуны (pri-goo-NI), "The Jumpers." They jump during their religious worship when moved by the Spirit.

The smaller group is called Постоянные (pos-to-YAN-nye) meaning, "The Steady Ones."

To this day, both groups keep some of the Orthodox forms of worship, with some modification. For example, the Russian word for "thank you" is spasibo (спасибо), meaning, "God save." The Molokans changed this form of "thank you" to Спаси Господь, (spa-see gos-PODj) "Lord save."

The Orthodox use the sign of the cross with three fingers. The Molokans use the same sign with the whole body—first they bow forward, and then to the right, then left, and finally to the rear.

Molokans do not believe in baptism. However, they perform a certain religious ceremony on infants and called it kstiny (кстины, ks-TEEN-ee). By the way, the word kstiny does not exist in the Russian language; it is a corrupt form of krestiny (крестины, kres-TEEN-ee) which means "child baptism."

There are other differences. The "Jumpers" follow the Old Testament Jewish holy days, such as Passover, adopting a mixture of Hebrew and Catholic traditions. They observe Passover on the same day the Jews do.

Furthermore, they celebrate the Day of the Tabernacle (Sukkot), the Day of Trumpets (Rosh Hashanah), the Day of Judgment (Yom Kippur), and Pentecost. The form of celebration is different. This group is more conservative. For example, men wear beards and do not sport neckties.

The "Steady" group, on the other hand, is more liberal. They follow mostly the Catholic calendar of holidays. Some men and women attend church in Western dress.

There were other, smaller religious groups that differed from the Molokans, such as in considering Saturday as the true day of worship. This group was named Subbotniki, which means "The Sabbatarians," like Seventh-day Adventists. Most of the Volkovs were Subbotniki, and there were four Seventh-day Adventist families who considered the Bible, and only the Bible, as a true rule of faith.

Later, a few Baptists and a family of Pentecostals arrived on the scene. Still later, a family of Orthodox believers also moved to our village.

*   *   *

One day, a Russian-speaking Adventist missionary appeared in Rahmatabad, with American

Adventist missionaries, in a car. They stopped by an Adventist family of our village, the Muravyovs.

The Muravyov family consisted of a widow, Tatyana Ilyinichna, with three adult sons, Vasiliy, Fyodor, and Aleksey, all three of whom had their own families. Tatyana, their mother, lived with Aleksey's family. She also had three daughters, Anna (Nura), Maria (Manya), and Evdokia (Dusya). Nura was married to a Molokan, Yakov Kashirsky; Manya was married to another Molokan, Pionsky. They lived in the city. Dusya was a teenager and lived with her mother and brother Aleksey.

The visiting Russian-speaking Adventist's name was Mikhail Semyonovich Beitzakhar (known as "Beitz" in the United States, pronounced "Bates" for short). He was by nationality an Assyrian. He was born in Persia, but due to political unrest, his family had moved to Russia. While there, he met a Russian girl, Anastasia Semyonovna, whom he married, and while there, he accepted the Adventist faith. He then attended the Adventist seminary in Kiev, Ukraine, and became a pastor.

After becoming acquainted with the Muravyovs, the American missionaries suggested to conduct religious sermons for the villagers.

The missionaries preached, and Elder Beitzakhar translated.

Every evening, after dark, they connected a projector to the car's battery and showed colored pictures outside on a stretched white sheet. With the help of visual aids, the Daniel's prophecies with strange beasts were fascinating and entertaining; besides, the mystery of Daniel's prophecies became understandable and convincing. As a result, more people came to this evangelism.

In any small community, a new arrival with new technology will spark curiosity. In no time, the news of strangers in the village spread throughout Rahmatabad. On Sabbath day, church was almost full.

The Beitzakhar's sermons were unusual, to say the least. He spoke in proper, educated Russian, yet with simple, understandable language. He backed his topics with proper stories. He wore glasses, dressed in a tailor-made three-piece suit and tie, and sported a Charlie Chaplin style toothbrush mustache. And he carried a camera.

To some attendees his speech was welcomed with great approval.

But others were very suspicious of him. For this latter group, anyone who spoke in educated language was looked upon as a lazy person or a crook. To them the only honest profession was physical labor.

He was instantly dubbed не наш (nee NAWSH), "not ours." The final factor for disapproval was his Assyrian heritage—not Russian. However, he was a soft-spoken, positive person and the young people were attracted to him. That posed a dangerous spiritual threat to those who were not Adventists.

Soon the Beitzakhar family moved to Rahmatabad, where Elder Beitzakhar was able to solidify most of the Subbotniki into one Adventist congregation. This led to construction of a house of worship. Though this structure was crude, with a thatched roof and dirt floor, the interior resembled a typical Protestant church with pews and a pulpit.

The church was built on the Muravyovs' property. Ivan Stepanovich Gudima, a man of all trades and a recent arrival to Rahmatabad from Ukraine, built the pews and the pulpit. Gudima was a dedicated Adventist and took this responsibility seriously. After all, he was to make something for God, so he applied his God-given gift to the best of his ability.

He crafted the furniture for the church to perfection. Even though this church, a worship structure of mud bricks and a sedge roof, didn't appear like a typical church, inside, it was a sanctuary. Gudima even constructed a raised platform for the pulpit.

The thatched-roof church had four glass windows, two on each side of the structure. Before window panes were installed, a pair of mud swallows built a nest. They took up residence on one of the beams, inside what was to be a house of worship. Church members felt that this pair of fowl was a gift from God. So, when the church members installed the window panes, they left a space big enough for the swallows to fly through.

I remember sitting beside my widowed mother on one of those pews observing how these diligent birds flitted in and out during church service. To me, their labor on Sabbath was far more interesting than a "boring" adult sermon. When fledglings hatched, my attention was glued to the study of nature. I was receiving more blessing from watching the "good luck" of God's creatures than by just listening to biblical lectures.

What amazed me most, besides observing the parents bringing insects to their young, was the fact that when the little critters would turn their butts toward the edge of the nest to relieve themselves, one of the parents was there to catch the unnecessary excess and carry it out the window.

I don't remember any miscarriage of their hygienic duty. After a short while, to my regret, the entertaining family would abandon their home. Soon enough to my joy, these adorable birds would come back the following season to bless me. To this day, I have special affection toward swallows.

I should mention the way the church members took care of this house of worship. All floors of village houses were made of mud and foot traffic created dust—a perfect breeding ground for fleas.

To prevent fleas, the women would combine clay and cow dung in water, then coat the floor with its mix. It is better to endure the smell than to put up with fleas. So, church members took turns cleaning and "disinfecting" our church every Friday.

Sabbath mornings, the Muravyovs would open the church doors to air out the place. The odor was worse during hot summers. Strange as it seems, with time, this noxious smell became associated with cleanliness. Besides, the clay helped minimize irritation of the olfactory senses.

The Adventist Church, Rahmatabad, with oak shingles on roof.

The Beitzakhars.

The original Subbotniki group, Iran. Mikhail Semyonovich
Beitzakhar at right in raincoat. At left, Nastya showing off her
firstborn son, Ivan.

Mikhail Semyonovich worked hard to solidify the *Subbotniki* and organize a well-functioned congregation, with distinct Biblical doctrines that conformed to and paralleled the worldwide Adventist movement. He was instrumental in organizing a public school with the support of the government, where he taught Russian and the Bible.

His oldest daughter, Luba, just under the age of twenty, had a government teaching credential and could teach other subjects. Soon, the government sent their own principal to our school. Now the Rahmatabad children could attend a local school, instead of having to trek to the one in Fazelabad all the way by the Shah's Highway.

With the prosperity of an Adventist community, more Russian-speaking Adventist families began to arrive from other parts of the country. From new arrivals, Adventist church members learned new Christian songs.

Soon, Pastor Beitzakhar had song books printed in Russian. These activities began to attract young people and the success of Elder Beitzakhar's religious labor became glaringly noticeable. That caused some dormant feelings of jealousy to sprout.

No matter how cultured or how spiritual we are, we human beings do not conquer all our character defects, one of which is jealousy. Somehow, we become uncomfortable when our rivals prosper—even in religion. These feelings may lie dormant deep inside of us, but given the right stimulus, they surface their ugly heads.

Other religious groups began to boycott the Adventist assemblies, and their elders discouraged their family members from attending these services. As if that wasn't enough, someone reported to Persian officials that Pastor Beitzakhar was an American spy.

To keep peace among residents in Rahmatabad, government officials demanded that the Beitzakhars leave the village. Consequently, they had to move to Gorgon, the nearest city some thirty miles away. They complied. Pastor Beitzakhar could only travel to Rahmatabad for special occasions.

By this time, our own Adventist church was organized, thanks to Elder Beitzakhar. Shortly thereafter, the Adventist Conference recalled him and directed him to another part of their mission field. This necessitated the Beitzakhar family to move to Teheran.

Chapter 33

Romance and Marriage

Marriage is the world's first institution established in Eden, when God presented Eve to Adam for the purpose of companionship, love and procreation. To this day, all societies (to my knowledge) have some form of marriage rites. Rahmatabad had its own form of culture in this area. First, let me mention one aspect that somehow impacted the lives of those refugees.

Some anthropologists suggest that on the average, more boys are born than girls, and even more boys are born under stressful conditions. If that is true, this phenomenon was certainly reflected in the lives of these refugees in a foreign land.

These people had their share of stress in abundance. Even though they felt some relief from Communist oppression, they experienced a different form of hardship: adapting to a life under an Islamic regime, learning a new language, and setting down new roots.

This situation brought mixed blessings: the young men were exempt from military service and none of them had participated in any wars. However, there was a disproportion of more young men than girls, which created a surplus of young men and a shortage of young women. This situation favored girls, because any female wearing a skirt, even with some handicap, was guaranteed a husband. As far as beauty is concerned, all Rahmatabad girls were beautiful.

Where life is arduous and entertainment options are in short supply, people crave for some interruption of the mundane flow of existence. Young people are very inventive—they find joy and pleasure in many ways. One form of entertainment they learned from their parents was the singing of folk songs; some of which were, somewhat, morally questionable. Nevertheless, these "questionable morals" of songs were overlooked. Dancing, on the other hand, was forbidden. It was considered too worldly, and, even sinful.

Teenagers organized themselves into exclusive groups by age, and occasionally by maturity. To join such a unit was not simple. There were rules and regulations that controlled the "sanctity" of these inner circles. One had to earn status, either by age or maturity.

On holidays after sundown, girls would walk together, arms locked, parading from one end of the only street in the village to the other, and back. Boys would follow behind, singing. Sometimes, they would play a form of "catch" games in the meadow. Other times, girls would get together and organize special dinners for the boys in someone's house, with the help of fun-loving mothers. After the "banquet," they would play some innocent games. "Spin the bottle," a form of a kissing game, was considered appropriate.

The boys had to return the favor with some modification—they would invite the girls to the forested mountains. In summer time, girls would bring lunch, and boys would bring watermelons, and chains.

They'd find a brook and put their watermelons into its cool water, while some agile boys would climb a tall oak tree and attach two chains side by side onto the oak limb. At the bottom end of the chains, they would hook a sturdy stick. The swing is ready.

The fun begins. A boy would invite a girl to stand with him on the stick, facing her partner with anticipation. The boy then would give his sweetheart the thrill of her life. First he would swing her slowly, then faster, and higher, as if on a trapeze, so high that they would rise almost parallel to the branch, while the girl would scream from delight or terror. Not all girls were brave enough to accept the thrilling invitation, unless the boy promised to swing the girl gently.

When we're young, we do some weird acts which we regret in later years. My brother, Mikhail, told me about a strange incident which I remember to this day.

One holiday afternoon, a group of young bachelors from our village decided to spend a day in the nearby forest just for fun. None of them thought of bringing something to eat, and as they idled through the forest, they came across an unattended flock of sheep.

Suddenly, they felt pangs of hunger and began to salivate. They looked around, and, not seeing anyone else in sight, they came to an idea on how to satiate their hunger—they decided to have shish cabob. The more they thought about barbequed lamb, the hungrier they became. And without further thought, they approached the flock of sheep and caught one.

Here, they faced a dilemma: who is to slaughter the animal?

One stepped forward and announced, "Ehhh," as if to say, "Finders, keepers. Losers, weepers. It's not a big crime."

He forced the sheep to the ground, got on his knees, and asked someone for a knife. Then he took his hat off. The rest followed suit. With weapon in hand, he was ready to perform the solemn ritual—recite the Lord's prayer, as the custom required.

One of the youths, with his hat still on, came up to the "butcher," kicked him in his posterior, and said, "You, *expletive*, stole something, and are now asking God to bless your crime?"

The slaughterer was so shocked that he let go of the victim, and the latter ran away bleating.

The bachelors went hungry.

Boys are more aggressive and more possessive than girls. Fortunately, they are more careful when approaching young ladies than in their approach to solitary sheep in the forest.

Back in the village, boys on either end of town claimed the girls in their neighborhood, even though the street was only a mile long. Each young person tried to marry the one belonging to his or her church. But, since there was more fun in larger groups, the youth played corporately. But, when romance was involved, that's where the border limits were firmly established. When these borders were violated, a fist fight loomed on the horizon.

Girls too competed for handsome boys. When a girl would spot a boy, who made her heart do somersaults, she would ask a trusted friend to relay her feeling to the object of her affection. The trusted friend would approach the "target" and coyly coo something like this: "I have a secret for you."

"Really? What kind of secret?" the boy would ask, with pretense of indifference.

"If I let you know, then it won't be a secret, will it?"

"OK, give me a hint."

"A beautiful girl thinks you're cute."

"Who is she?" queries the boy.

"Just watch and I'll give you some signs." The romance has been germinated.

This romantic shoot would sprout and grow. The girl would make a handkerchief, embroidered with colorful thread, sometimes even adding the boy's initials onto it. She'd wash and iron it, then fold it with the utmost care, and insert it into a homemade envelope. It was ready for her liaison to present it to her heartthrob.

A shy girl had better grab the romantic reins into her own hands. Otherwise, the trusted friend may turn out to be a traitor. Who knows, the saying "everything's fair in love and war" may become more than just a saying.

When the boy accepts the meaningful gift, he displays it in his shirt pocket as a trophy for everyone to see. Flattered, the boy struts around demonstrating to everyone that he is claimed. From then on, the couple begins to share each other's company on all social occasions.

One time, my bashful, towheaded sister, Nadya, who later married Pavel Gorbenko, crocheted a handkerchief for some future boyfriend. She washed it and spread it on a bush to dry. A boy she couldn't stand happening to pass by, and seeing the hanky, he surreptitiously appropriated it.

Later, this "brute" displayed his trophy in his shirt pocket and secured it with a safety pin. Still later, and in public, Nadya saw her purloined precious possession in the pocket of the thief. She approached him with trepidation and then yanked her precious property so hard she ripped his shirt, letting him know that she was not, and never intended to be, his girlfriend. Suddenly, this quiet girl became noticeable.

No matter how hard the youth devised creative means in selecting future life companions, the last word of the matter rested in the hands of parents, or even grandparents. Most of the time, parents did go along with their children's choices. However, there were occasions when parents would announce, "Over my dead body!" Such tragic situations caused tragic consequences. I know of only two elopements.

Let's say the hopes of a happy pair have materialized. A new phase then enters the lives of many others as well: their parents, relatives, and, most of all, their friends. They select a beloved trusted adult woman as ambassador to relay the news to their parents.

Next, the groom's parents, together with the matchmaker, dress in their holiday garb and approach the (hopefully) future bride's parents. The young woman's parents are forewarned of this entourage. They too are ready to welcome the honored guests. The house is clean: everything is in order, both inside and out. The dirt floor is swept, the beds are decorated with the best bedspreads, and square pillows are stacked pyramid fashion at the head of the bed. After all, the condition of the house is a reflection on the bride-to-be.

Appear the suitors with the words, *Мир дому вашему* (meer do-moo vashe-moo) "Peace to your home." They are graciously welcomed with *С миром принимаем* (s mirom pree-nee-MA-yem), "With peace we welcome you." Guests are seated and small talk ensues.

Finally, the main purpose of this delicate mission is breached. Here begins the bartering for a bride. After nervous coughing, the father of the intended groom opens with the initial well-rehearsed offer, "Vasiliy Ivanich and Maria Petrovna, we have come to you with a delicate mission."

"And what kind of mission is that, may we know, Aleksey Grigorich?" banters the father of the intended bride, presenting a facade of total ignorance of the mission.

Both parties know full well why they are here and what each wants, but this game of fox and fowl has to run its course. It has "rules" that everyone hates to engage in, but they must be adhered to.

Aleksey Grigorich comes to the point, "Vasiliy Ivanich, my wife Tatyana Andreyevna and I have come to ask for the hand of your daughter, Natalia Vasilyevna, to marry our son Andrey Alekseyich." Formality is one of the "must" rules of the game.

"Aleksey Grigorich, my wife Maria Petrovna and I are flattered with your proposal, but our daughter Natalia Vasilyevna is too young to marry, she's only seventeen."

"Already seventeen!" exclaims Tatyana Andreyevna, intimating as if Natalia is entering the stage of old maid. "I was sixteen when I married Aleksey Grigorich."

At this moment, the master matchmaker prevents a possible miscarriage of the "deal". She declares, "Age seventeen is a perfect time for a girl to marry."

And she begins to extol the virtues of Andrey—that he is a hard worker, he attends church regularly, he never uses foul language, and doesn't smoke or drink. He loves Natalia and would make a perfect husband for her. In other words, Andrey is ready for canonization. Besides, she adds, both Natalia and Andrey would make a match blessed by Heaven.

Both sets of parents have already made up their minds for the wedding to go through; however, they are compelled to see the rules of this game all the way through, and must bring it to its ultimate culmination. Once the agreement is made, the bride is summoned.

Natalia walks in dressed in her best garment, bashful, eyes downcast.

She is to face another prescribed tradition—bestowal of the blessings. The intended bride kneels in front of her parents. The parents place their right hand on their daughter's head and recite an appropriate passage of scripture. That done, the daughter is now spoken for. The wedding is set for fall, after crops are harvested.

When this news is broadcasted, many events explode with frenzied rapidity in the community. It's like eggs in a nest—when one chick hatches, the rest follow suit. The young people go into panic mode.

The situation resembles a department store going out of business, or like the American "Black Friday." There's a frenzied rush to get the best before all the merchandise disappears. Girls are like sale items, all prettied and placed in the most noticeable spots. Though the girls traditionally waited to be proposed to, some are clever and devious enough to invent the right bait to attract the desired catch. Soon, the community "nest" is empty.

Very rarely, someone is overlooked. Such unfortunate youth can be an orphan, from a poor family, or of another faith.

There used to be a custom, a vestige from Orthodoxy. At the marriage ceremony, if the bride and groom are of different religious faith, the bride would promise to accept the groom's faith.

Naturally, each young person prefers to marry someone of similar denomination. For several reasons, this preference doesn't always work out. And because a young girl does not want to remain an old maid, she will marry the one who proposes to her.

If a girl was not deeply convinced of her religious leaning, marrying someone of another faith posed no serious problem; the couple can cultivate happiness. On the other hand, if a girl's religious conviction was deeply rooted, that could bring to pass a lifetime of unhappiness and misery. And divorce was far worse than remaining an unmarried woman.

Chapter 34

Nadya's Wedding

Let me tell you about my sister Nadya's marriage. Nadya had soft blond hair and light blue eyes, the color of flowering flax field in bloom. She had several admirers but she ignored them all, mostly because of her religion—she was a Seventh-day Adventist.

One day, a family appeared in Rahmatabad; a father, Ivan Zinoveyevich Gorbenko, and his two handsome boys in their early twenties, Pavel and Gregory. They were Adventists from the Ukraine.

The Gorbenkos lived in the forest, where they kept an apiary. Pavel, the older of the two, was literate with some scholastic leaning. Gregory, of middle height, was well proportioned in bodily and facial features. Being muscular and athletic, and with acrobatic skills, he would have made a perfect model for a classical Greek god. His tuft of hair just above his forehead made him even more attractive.

He was always flocked by children asking him if they could feel his biceps, or they begged him to do acrobatic tricks. He always obliged. Sometimes he would take a couple of walnuts out of his pocket, arrange them in the crook of his arm, and flex his biceps—crack would go the walnuts. The boys' eyes would almost pop out of their orbits. The kids thought of him as some "superman." Though physically he was the epitome of perfection, socially and scholastically he was wanting.

Gregory's brother Pavel, on the other hand, was taller, and socially personable. He was a good storyteller. He sang baritone and participated in some church activities. Later in his life, the church nominated him to the post of head eldership.

The citizenry of the village did not accept these brothers. First off, they were of different faith, they were Ukrainian, and they were not farmers. Also, the young people of the village looked at them as threats and guarded their females with intense jealousy. After all, there was a deficit in the number of girls.

One day, Ivan Zinoveyevich came to our house and asked to see Mama and Aleksey privately (as Aleksey was the oldest male in the family). Ignoring all conventions, and with a business-like manner, Ivan Zinoveyevich came directly to the point—a proposal of marriage between our youngest daughter Nadya, not quite seventeen, and his son, Pavel Gorbenko. Though Pavel was much older than Nadya, the match seemed good.

Both were Adventists and both were of good standing in the church; besides, there was no one else more suitable. Although there were some young men among the non-Adventists, Nadya was choosy.

Nadya was summoned into the presence of Ivan Zinoveyevich. Mama broke the news, and then asked Nadya what she thought about it. My sister gave her assent. The father-in-law-to-be reached for his pocket and produced an envelope, which he offered to his future daughter-in-law. Nadya, surprised and confused, just held it in her hands.

"Open it," urged Ivan.

She gingerly opened it. The contents revealed a gold wedding band. Nadya was at a loss of what to do with it. This was out of the ordinary. Such convention was entirely new to her—to present a future bride with any kind of ring, let alone a gold one. Yes, some girls did sport some cheap trinkets—as a toy.

This item had meaning, Nadya was flabbergasted. It was a form of dowry. To avoid making an issue, at such a momentous time in the life of her daughter, Mama said nothing. Neither did Aleksey.

"Try it on. See if it fits," suggested her potential, hopeful father-in-law.

Nadya tried it and it fit just right.

The time for wedding preparation commenced.

Meanwhile, one Sunday afternoon, when Nadya was already spoken for, and when she and I were returning home from the fields, a handsome young man (from an Orthodox family) accosted us.

Falling on his knees in front of Nadya, he begged her to break the engagement with her intended, Pavel Gorbenko, and marry him instead. He began promising her mountains of gold. Nadya, in her wildest imagination, had never even dreamed of, or expected such display of attention and affection.

After all, she was only a country girl of seventeen. She was completely astonished. She backed away from him, and he crawled toward her on his knees. She then turned around and dashed away from him like a gazelle, leaving him on his haunches. I thought it was one hilarious comedy, but I didn't dare open my mouth, let alone tease her.

On the eve of her wedding, Nadya's girlfriends arranged a farewell, all-night party for her. When everyone lay to sleep on the floor, and then fell asleep, this slighted suitor tiptoed into the house with scissors. Finding sleeping Nadya, he very gingerly snipped a lock of her golden hair, right in front of her forehead.

In that moment, she stirred, and the hair-snipping rat dashed away disappearing into darkness. He had dropped his weapon, leaving the scissors to identify the romantic criminal. These were not ordinary scissors. They were expensive, the kind that only professionals use. You see, his sister was a professional seamstress. She had been asked to sew Nadya's wedding dress and was at the farewell party that night.

I believe that probably, the siblings were in cahoots. In the morning, when the weapon was found, everyone suspected their true owner. However, the sister vehemently denied that she'd ever laid her eyes on those scissors, let alone owned them.

Nothing was ever done about it. Nadya was too embarrassed to broadcast the escapade throughout the village on her wedding day. To compensate for the ordeal, Nadya became the possessor of the expensive, professional item—a souvenir of her encounter with the slighted vengeful romantic.

When Nadya was being attired for her marriage ceremony, someone managed to camouflage the evidence of the ravished hair cleverly so that no one noticed the deficit in her golden locks.

My sister, Nadya.

On their wedding day, Pavel Gorbenko and Nadya with ravished flocks.

Chapter 35

Persian Peasant Wedding

Come along with me to a Persian wedding. It was a warm, beautiful, autumn Sunday. I was finishing up the task of cleaning livestock stalls, when I heard the rhythmical beats of a distant drum and a piercing shrill of a pipe called "zurna."

I instantly recognized the meaning of the festive sound, the procession of a Persian wedding. I flung remaining cow dung out the door, ran home, and tossed my shoes under my bed. I announced to my mother, "Mama, I'm going to watch the wedding procession," and, without waiting for a comment from her, dashed out of the house barefoot as if released from shackles.

The wedding procession was coming from Aliabad, a village south of Rahmatabad. Our house was the last house on the southern end of our village. I had a close friend, Ivan Muravyov, who lived only half way down the only village street.

Instead of waiting for the joyous procession alone, I sped along the dusty street toward Ivan, feeling the powdery dust squeezing between my toes.

Ivan was already there, standing, waiting for me. I was one year older than Ivan.

Soon, the noisy celebrants approached our observation point. First, came musicians and dancers. Then, followed the groom on horseback, accompanied by other riders, some with shotguns. Finally in tow, were pedestrian idlers.

As the procession passed by, we joined the gawkers, hopping and skipping toward Fazelabad, a village on the Shah's highway, inhabited by both Russians and Persians. It was the home of the bride.

Arriving in Fazelabad, a mile or so, we were swept along with the groom's party, headed for the bride's house, where another crowd—mostly women and children—waited impatiently. The groom's procession stopped and solemn silence ensued.

A middle-aged man, dismounted from his steed and approached the residence of the bride, a brick house with a thatched roof. Out came another man, presumably the father of the bride or some close relative. The first man bowed to the second, saying, "*Salam Alaikum.*"

"*Alaikum Salam,*" responded the second man.

"We have come to claim the bride. Is she ready?"

"She is ready. Have you brought the final payment as agreed?"

"*Bali, agha* (Yes, sir), we have," answered the groom's father, handing over something bundled inside a kerchief.

The host ceremoniously untied the dowry, exposing its contents—brand new crisp, paper currency. He counted the money and nodded his approval.

As if on cue, the crowd backed away, and the entertainers struck up music, once again.

A father and four sons were the only musicians in this area, who were hired for various festivities. The chief musician was the father, a tall, lanky old man with a long, thin face, long black teeth, and a cataract on his left eye. He played a three-stringed instrument with a long neck protruding from a gourd-shaped base resembling a miniature drum. This instrument was balanced on a single leg, resembling a cello. He played it by rapidly moving the bow across the strings in short rapid strokes as he squatted on the ground.

One of his sons played the zurna. Another, in his early twenties, produced an intricate rhythm on a drum, creating different pitches by striking the drum with varied force of palms and fingers.

The youngest, a boy of no more than ten, beat a steady rhythm on a large drum. But the main attraction was the fourth son, a young man in his late teens who moved to the pulsating rhythm of the music in a whirling series of dance steps, cartwheels, and somersaults, punctuated by the jingly-jing of little metal plates attached to his thumb and fingers.

The crowd stood in a circle and kept the rhythm by snapping their fingers Persian style, using both hands, one palm over the other. This is accomplished by the right index finger, sliding off the left finger and striking against the rest of the other fingers, producing loud snaps. It helps if the index fingers are wet with saliva.

Several of the men from the crowd burst into the circle and began snapping their fingers over their heads, swinging their hips to the right, and left, with each snap chanting *"Beshkan! Beshkan!"* Crack it! Crack it!

Suddenly, in the middle of this excitement, a gunshot paralyzed the crowd, and diverted everyone's attention from the dancers in the circle, to the entrance of the house. Two women emerged leading the bride by her hands. Except for two narrowly netted slits, one for her eyes and the other for her nose, she was completely covered with a white sack-like fabric, known as *chodur*.

The three women stopped in front of the door. From behind them came a man and a couple of boys, each holding a bowl in the crook of one hand. They reached into the bowls and took a handful of something, then tossed it into the air.

Coins! Pandemonium broke out. Men, women, boys, girls—barefooted and shod—pulled, shoved, dragged, screamed, and leaped into the air as each shower of coins descended upon them.

The crowd resembled a flock of starlings fighting over earthworms in the furrow behind a plowman. One instant they would leap into the air with their hands outstretched, the next, they would scramble on all fours, grasping handfuls of dust, hoping to find some coins. Then they would leap into the air again. Those who tossed the largesse laughed with glee.

"Why are we standing, here, doing nothing? Let's get in there too," suggested Ivan.

"Let's! Here we go!" I shouted. And we dived into the churning crowd.

No sooner had we entered the press, than the shower of copper and silver stopped. The noise subsided, except for the sobbing and groaning of children who were caught in the melee. However, each of us had a coin in the hand mixed with dust.

As if on command, the crowd moved back and formed a wide aisle into which the two women led the bride, on either side of her. The attending women were dressed in their native holiday attire—long, wide, divided skirts and tunic-like blouses made from brightly colored, coarse, homespun raw silk, adorned with two rows of graduated silver coins from various countries. The coins were sewn onto the blouse in the shape of a "V", beginning with small coins at each shoulder and increasing in size as they descended, ending at the waistline with a large silver coin depicting some royal potentate.

The groom, a young fellow in his late teens, stepped into the aisle from the other end. Slightly taller and lankier than average, he was dressed in a striped brown double-breasted European jacket, homemade pants of gray fabric, which resembled the bottoms of men's pajamas, and oxford shoes. He marched purposefully down the aisle followed by a woman holding a mirror, which she held over her head, facing the bride's direction.

The two parties approached each other in total silence. Then the groom turned around and led the bride's attendees toward the horse over which the groom's father was mounted.

There the groom stopped and waited for his bride as she was led toward the same beast, as the woman with the mirror followed the bride. As they neared the horse, the groom smiled and stretched out his arms to help the bride atop the horse. But to his embarrassing surprise, one of the attending women to the bride, the one with the most coins and the one who displayed a huge silver coin with an imposing portrait of Her Majesty the Empress of the English Empire, Queen Victoria, pushed the groom rudely aside. The groom's visage transformed into a threatening ire.

With the help of the rider, the two women hauled the bride up onto the horse and positioned her behind her father-in-law to be. As the bride sat on the horse, her feet were exposed, revealing white patent leather shoes and white bobby socks.

As if to save the groom from his predicament, a young man stepped out of the crowd and headed toward him. As he approached the slighted star of the celebration, he leaned his head toward the groom as if to tell him something and then walked on without slowing down.

Suddenly another gunshot rang in the air. The groom, regaining his composure, dashed toward his own horse and, like a circus clown, leapt onto his mount and left the embarrassing spot.

All those who had horses followed suit, and the wedding procession retraced the same steps through Rahmatabad, heading on to Aliabad.

This second procession was twice the size of the first. The same musicians led the procession. The groom followed. Then rode the woman on horseback, still holding the mirror as before.

Next, followed the bride, positioned behind her future father-in-law. Finally, the other riders and pedestrians closed in the rear. Those who had shot guns fired them periodically, adding to the cacophony of the crowd.

Upon reaching Aliabad, the noisy procession headed directly for a public bathhouse, where they stopped. An older woman confronted them, and everyone dismounted. With loving care, the women helped the bride off the horse and into the bathhouse.

"What's happening now?" I asked the bystanders, but they gave me an unwelcome look and walked away.

"They're examining the bride's virginity." We turned around and saw a shabbily dressed, odd-looking man.

The villagers who had heard the comment gave the old man dirty looks. I felt awkward. After all, we were outsiders. Yet, we could not overcome our curiosity. We sheepishly hobbled away and sat under a mulberry tree, awaiting the momentous decision with keen anticipation.

Suddenly we were startled by cheerful shouts. We looked up and saw the groom and the bride—who still looked like a cocoon wrapped in her wedding trappings—walking side by side, along a path leading to the village mosque. Since Christians are barred from Moslem mosques, we returned home to ruminate over our strange discovery.

When we arrived home, we were pleasantly surprised to learn that our families had received invitations to the wedding feast at the groom's house.

Not wanting to miss any of the fun, we set off at once to the groom's hut some distance from Aliabad. When we came to the appointed place, we realized that we had come too early. However, there were already many curious young Persian villagers who had forestalled us.

We stood to one side and observed the restless anticipators. Some of them scrambled up mulberry and poplar trees to be the first to view the joyous advent of the newlyweds. From their vantage point, they reported every move on the dusty road. Frequently, they raised the anticipation of the crowd below with false alarms.

Ivan noticed a familiar figure to one side of the crowd. "Hey, Yashka, do you recognize that man over there?" He motioned with his head, nodding towards three young men who stood casually, talking amongst themselves, as if they were in a world of their own.

"Yeah, that's the fellow who whispered something to the groom after the woman pushed him away. He has two friends with him. I wonder what they are up to." I couldn't help but to keep an eye on them. I felt they had some plot.

Suddenly there was an explosion of shouts from the boys in the trees, "They're coming! They're coming!" They slid down from their observation points and dashed down the dusty road to meet the long-expected party.

The distant shrill sounds of the pipe ensued, and festive drum beats reached our ears. The familiar sound created more excitement among the waiting crowd. The three comrades did not share the excitement. They just looked casually toward the speeding boys and continued with their conspiracy.

Soon the procession, in the same order—mirror and all—headed toward the groom's residence, lacking the morning exuberance. When the tired celebrants approached their destination, they stopped their procession. So did the music.

The dusty road was cleared of people, leaving the groom, the bride, and the two women in attendance in the middle of the road.

I felt some mysterious anticipation in the crowd. The three conspirators elbowed themselves through the crowd and stood in front of the line, smiling. Ivan's and my curiosity heightened, as we raised ourselves on our tiptoes and peered over the heads of spectators in front of us.

A man approached the groom, carrying a hat in his hands. He carefully handed it to the groom and then ran back to the crowd, as if the thing was about to explode. The groom accepted the hat and gently placed it in the crook of his left hand.

The bride, still hidden in her wedding *chodur,* was positioned in the middle of the road with her arms outstretched. The attending women held her arms on both sides, also outstretching theirs.

The groom measured twenty paces away from the bride and stopped. He surveyed the spectators, enjoying the attention he received. Reaching into the hat, he produced an object from the hat and waved it to the public. An egg. Holding the egg, he ceremoniously stretched his hand toward the bride.

Squinting one eye, he aimed at the bride and threw it awkwardly at her. Ivan and I gasped with incredulity. The egg flew over the heads of the women, who unsuccessfully tried to catch it with their hands. The egg plumped into the soft dust far behind the bride and splashed.

The crowd booed and laughed—except the three young men. They looked at each other, smiling, and whispered something. I was sure they had planned something, but what, I couldn't surmise.

The groom, going through the same motions, sent another egg on its course. This time the egg flew faster and barely missed the bride. Another plump in the dust, another wave of jeers.

Now, the groom assumed a different manner. He reached for the last egg. He tossed the hat to one side, and slowly panned the audience, as if searching for someone. Then, his gaze stopped. Facing his coconspirators, he smiled and slightly nodded his head. His friends nodded in response.

Silence ensued. The crowd held its corporate breath.

The groom theatrically turned his back toward his wife. Then, like lightning, he pivoted on his heels and sent the oval missile on its course with fury. Before anyone could realize what had happened, the projectile struck the bull's eye. The woman's Queen Victoria coin was the target. It exploded like a gunshot. It splattered his nemesis' colorful costume, adding more color to her wardrobe.

The bystanders were beside themselves. The three-party troika doubled with laughter. We were dumbfounded.

The object of the broom's vengeance, dripping with slime, was furious. Her eyes became narrow slits. Her lips tightened as if pulled on a string. Her temple kept popping out like a bullfrog's when it croaks. She jerked the bewildered bride by the hand, and dragged her toward the groom's house. The other attendants hobbled after, shaking their heads.

"What happened?" I asked some boys near me. "Why are they throwing eggs at the bride?"

They could hardly speak for laughter. One of the older boys said, "It's the custom, her ..." And the boys burst into another bout of laughter. Between speaking and laughing, the boys explained that if the groom hits the bride, or one of the two women, the marriage would be happy." But no groom wants to hit his bride," added one boy. "As long as he hits one of the three, it counts."

"That's why the women tried to catch the eggs," commented Ivan.

"That's right."

"Then it's okay for the groom to hit the woman with an egg?" I added.

"Yes, but not that hard." Again, the boys were attacked with a fit of laughter, as if they had just witnessed a hilarious drama. Then, they joined the happy procession.

I didn't think throwing eggs at a bride was funny. We turned around and headed home.

Chapter 36

A Persian Wedding Feast

When we arrived home, we found out that the wedding feast would start in the late afternoon. Ivan didn't even go home. We invited him to stay and have a light lunch. We could hardly wait until the start of the feast. We decided to go there earlier. Before we even arrived at the scene of the feast, I could smell the aroma of barbecued lamb.

Even though I had eaten just recently, my mouth began to water as soon as I smelled the familiar pungent aroma of Persian shish kebab. Without realizing it, we increased our pace and then started running.

When we reached the wedding site, we were out of breath and very hungry. We could see people scurrying frantically, hither and thither, applying last touches to the feast. There were several mangals with crude grills over hot charcoals, upon which sizzled choice chunks of mutton.

Soon, guests began to arrive and sit upon mats and rugs spread around the yard. A few Russian women appeared on the scene, too. These were ushered to one corner of the yard and seated upon a colorful Persian rug.

We were not interested in anything other than watching the men who tended to the kebab. We couldn't tear our eyes from the scores of skewers, fascinated. We watched the meat placed on red-hot charcoals, where it slowly turned bronze, out of which oozed pearls of spicy juices dripping onto fire. The drops sizzled and transformed into thin blue smoke that wafted gently through the air, making my mouth drool. When both sides of the kebab turned brown, the delicious delicacies were slid off the skewers onto mountains of generously buttered white rice.

Everything seemed exaggerated out of proportion, including our appetites. Piles of pilaf were sprinkled with dried, ground pomegranates, turmeric, saffron, and some other exotic spices, and passed in huge bowls to guests. Locals took small portions of kebab with their fingers, mixing them with rice and making small balls, which they dexterously shot into their mouths.

Finally, a similar bowl of shish kebab was brought to the Russian corner. Very patiently, each Russian guest reached into their pockets and produced a handkerchief, wrapped around spoons. Each person took their spoon out, murmured a short prayer, "In the name of the Father, and the Son and the Holy Ghost, Amen," and dug into the mountain of mouth-watering ivory grains.

Oh, horrors of horrors! We had no spoons! Being in the middle of a fabulous feast and not able to taste any food was more than we could bear. I was on the verge of tears. Then my mother reached into the other pocket of her skirt, and produced two more spoons and handed them to us with a significant smile that seemed to say, "Oh, you poor creatures, what would you do without your mothers?"

What a relief! We lost all control of ourselves. We even dispensed with a short prayer. All we could muster was to force ourselves to say "Amen," and attacked the pilaf as if it were an enemy. We devoured it like hungry wolves. Oh, I had tasted all kinds of kebab with all sorts of spices, but this kebab was fit for the Greek gods. It was light like air, perfectly seasoned, and incredibly easy to eat.

Before we realized it, the pilaf disappeared, and the feast was over. The sun had just hidden behind Bald Mountain, and dusk was rapidly thickening.

The bride was led out of the house, where she was sequestered with her attendants during the entire feast, while the groom enjoyed his meal in the company of his three co-conspirators, talking and laughing. This was now the time for the women. Some of the men stood in peripheries and observed the women's world, while others tended to leftovers.

Still cocooned in her *chodur*, the bride was seated on a stool. One attendant took the bride's right hand and placed it on top of her head, palm upward. I noticed a round yellow spot dyed in the middle of her tiny palm, a sign of beauty.

The other woman picked up each present, one at a time, and place it on the bride's palm, which she held over her head, and named the gifts loudly—coins or some homespun silk fabrics. She then waved each gift to the seated audience and placed them behind the bride for safekeeping. If the gift was too large to be placed on the hand, the master of ceremonies placed her own palm on top of the bride's head and announced the gift.

Some guests gave silk blouses with a few silver coins sewn onto them, and some gave lambs. Poorer guests gave rice, raisins, flour, and other produce. Russian girls gave embroidered handkerchiefs, trimmed with pretty lace.

With the presentation of gifts over, guests sauntered back to their homes in the dark.

Finally, the groom appeared on the scene. He gently put his arm around his new wife and led her into the house.

Family proceeded with clean up.

Soon, all traces of the feast vanished, except for the lingering fragrance of burnt meat in the air and on the branches of mulberry trees.

Family members stumbled into their dark house and quietly groped in darkness, feeling for their assigned place of rest.

Eventually the arms of Morpheus embraced the earthlings and led them to the land of Nod.

But not all of them.

Part VIII

Chapter 37

Education

Soon after we were settled in Rahmatabad, the villagers began to think about furthering their children's education. The problem? There were no teachers. And those who were literate, mostly men, had to provide a livelihood for their families. Besides, there was no building big enough to fit many children. God provided a teacher.

A family arrived to Rahmatabad. They were Baptists—the only ones in the whole village. They were not farmers and had no other source of income. Why they came to Rahmatabad, no one knew, and no one asked. This family was musically gifted and even had a pump organ—a rare novelty in the village. In no time, this family attracted young people who learned Christian songs, different from the ones they sang in their worship services. The husband of the family was educated.

Somehow, the elders of the village swallowed their pride and approached him with a proposition of teaching their brood reading, writing and arithmetic. The man agreed. The deal was settled: his payment would be mostly in farm produce. The head of the village, Vasiliy Trafimovich Konovalov, offered a part of his house for a classroom, containing a long table and crude benches. Due to lack of space, enrollment was limited—only teenagers were eligible.

More than anything else, I yearned for education, but because I was too young, I was rejected. I wanted so much to be included in the privileged group that I begged and cried. Mama went to the teacher and explained to him my insistence. She asked him if he would only let me stay in class and pretend I didn't exist. The teacher agreed. I was flying above the birds and above the clouds.

Keep in mind, this story occurs in a developing country. Fountain and ballpoint pens hadn't been invented. Chalk and blackboards were unheard of in our village. The only implement of writing in our village were regular and indelible pencils.

Like in Leo Tolstoy's story, "Filipok" (of whom I had never heard before that time), I sat on the floor, yoga style, at the entrance into the "classroom." Like a spider in a corner at daytime, I sat there, afraid to breathe, lest I would be expelled from this heavenly-sent privilege, and sponged knowledge avidly.

There were no primers. Luckily, someone during the escape thought about fetching some schoolbooks. To teach pupils alphabets, the teacher wrote alphabet letters on paper and, pointing to each letter, named it and asked the students to repeat after him.

I repeated every letter under my breath—fearing expulsion. If someone couldn't remember the name of a letter, the teacher would say, "Who knows what letter this is? Raise your hand." I knew every letter. Oh, how I wanted not only to raise my hand—I wanted to jump up and recite the whole alphabet, but dared not.

Not all the pupils who sat at the privileged table were interested in education, especially the older ones. I remember I was mad, as some of the big boys who didn't want to be there, repeating alphabet letters after someone not of their faith. They occupied precious space at the table, while I, who cried to be there, was relegated to sitting on the floor. What was worse, as I sat on the floor, I had a unique vantage point that was hidden from the teacher. I could see boys teasing girls and making obscene gestures under the table, and I couldn't do a thing about it. I didn't dare jeopardize my presence there.

From my early years, I learned two lessons: 1) If you want something bad enough and sacrifice something for it, like your pride, you'll obtain it, and 2) People are not what they appear on the surface—there is another side of them that could be ugly.

This discovery made me somewhat jaded and distrustful of others—especially of those children whose parents were in power.

This school didn't last long. For some reason, it fell apart. In a couple of years, when I was ten, a government school opened in Fazelabad along the Shah's highway, a couple of miles from where we lived. In this school, we were introduced to inkwells, steel pens, chalk, and even a chalkboard. The chalk came in lumps.

School attendance was mandatory. Any parent of school-age children who kept his kids in the fields, received corporal punishment.

One day, I witnessed such a corrective measure. One student regularly missed school. The teacher, who was also the principal, sent the school custodian, who was also our physical education instructor, to find out the reason for this student's absence from school. The custodian reported that the pupil was in the fields with his father. The principal delegated the PE teacher to bring the father to school.

When the father arrived, the principal lined up all the students on the exercise ground to witness the application of the education switch. Anticipating the pleasure of inducing pain on someone, the custodian had already prepared some mulberry switches. I have found that people with lower intellect enjoy destroying things and applying pain to others—animals included.

The principal ordered the father to lie down on the ground in supine position (on his back), face upward, and to take his shoes off and lift his bare feet with soles up. The teacher ordered the custodian to strike the father's bare feet with switches. The executioner performed his assignment with relish. After several strikes, the principal shouted, "Enough!"

I was aghast, especially when I noticed the father's wet pants, and his son screamed. Some students averted their eyes from the sad scene. I was so angry, I felt like dashing toward the custodian, grabbing the extra switch from the ground and letting him taste his own medicine.

Had Mama been there, she would have broken the switches to shreds on the executioner, including the principal. The schoolmaster blew his whistle, and students returned to their classes, leaving the humiliated man lying in the field. He was either too sore to walk or too embarrassed to rise and show his wet pants. This scene impressed the onlookers what will happen to fathers who kept their brood from attending school. After this graphic ordeal, school attendance noticeably improved.

Just a few years after this incident is when the Beitzakhar family had moved to Rahmatabad. Elder Beitz was instrumental in having a schoolhouse built in our village. Initially, he taught Russian language and arithmetic. His oldest daughter, Luba, had a governmental teaching certificate and taught Farsi. Later, she taught arithmetic.

The non-Adventist elders, for some reason, decided to "report" Elder Beitzakhar to government officials as an "American Spy." To prevent further complication, the officials ordered his involuntary move to Gorgon. In his place, they sent one of their own teachers who taught all subjects in Farsi. This move brought demise to education in the Russian language.

Chapter 38

Health Management

In Rahmatabad, and in surrounding areas, there were no professional physicians. Some of the villagers had various healing skills. For example, there were midwives, bonesetters (orthopedists) and "dermatologists." We even had a veterinarian who was also a "whisperer" or a charmer—to name a few. Some of these healers relied on natural sources like plantain, nettles, willow, garlic, cobweb, salt, butter, bees, even saliva.

Some remedies were purchased: iodine, castor oil, aspirin, opium, kerosene, and bluing. On rare occasions, some villagers turned to local Persian healers for charms and incantations. Bee stings and nettles were used to treat rheumatism. An adult patient suffering from a severe case of rheumatism is covered with a protective suit, except for legs, and placed directly in front of the beehive entrance.

Then the patient taps on the hive, causing the angry bees to sting the bare legs of the sick subject.

Another method of treating rheumatism is this way: The naked patient enters the steamy sauna, and after a few minutes, he or she is struck with a bunch of nettles on the back. The cure is successful, if the patient survives.

Bleeding stops when cobwebs are applied to cuts. Garlic is used on everything that ails you. Plantain, *подорожник* (podorozhnik), speeds healing on cuts, abrasions, and skin infections. Saliva is good for itching. Salt—for colds and flu.

Here is how I was treated for cholera. Among many chores, I had to herd calves. One late spring day after a good rain, I spent a good portion of a Friday in the field with young bovines. Toward the late afternoon, the weather turned quite warm, and I became very thirsty. I thought I'd die from dehydration. On the muddy road, in a small hollow from an animal's hoof, I saw some rainwater. I laid my handkerchief over the puddle, and using it as a filter, sipped the polluted water through it.

The following Sunday, my brother Mikhail took me haying with him. We set up camp. At the campsite, there was already a haystack. My job was to do "housekeeping," during the day. Suddenly, I felt discomfort in my stomach, weakness in my legs, slight dizziness, and nausea.

Without saying anything to my brother, I managed to fix supper; however, the smell of food made my stomach feel even more sick. I forced myself to swallow some food. Without mentioning my discomfort to Mikhail, hoping it would go away soon, I put supper items away and told my brother I needed to go to bed early. I scrambled up the haystack feeling worse. Usually, I enjoyed the pleasant aroma of the sun-dried hay—but not that evening.

In the middle of the night, I was attacked by leg and stomach cramps, vomiting, followed by diarrhea. I slid off my haystack and barely made it to the bushes. I headed back to mount my bed perch, but before I reached the top, the pains returned with vengeance. Back to the bushes.

After a few treks to the weeds, I was so weak I couldn't climb to my bed. I stayed below with my pants unbuttoned. By morning, just as dawn made objects distinguishable, I called for Mikhail and told him I was sick.

He quickly ran toward me, took one look at me, and without saying a word, dashed to the horses, hitched them to the wagon, picked me up, laid me on the wagon, covered me with a blanket, and galloped home.

When Mikhail reached home, Mama was already up. Sensing the danger, she ran to Mikhail and asked the reason for such haste.

"Yashka is sick," said Mikhail.

Mama flung the blanket off me and gasped. Always resourceful, Mama sprung to action.

"Get Ghulam!" She commanded my already exhausted brother.

Ghulam was the herdsman who drove our cattle across the border during our flight from Soviet Russia. The white-haired healer followed behind Mikhail. He was retired by this time, and lived at the edge of the village with his wife and an adopted Russian orphan whom he loved dearly.

Meanwhile, Mama and sister Nadya pulled me off the wagon, cleaned me up and made me comfortable.

On the way, Mikhail explained to Ghulam my condition.

"What happened?" Ghulam asked me in a husky voice.

In a shaky voice, I relayed my ordeal during the night.

"What did you eat yesterday?" he asked.

"Whatever Mama fixed. I don't remember," I answered.

"Did you eat or drink anything recently that was different from other days?"

Then, I remembered drinking polluted water from an animal's hoof hollow.

"You got cholera, Yasha," Ghulam announced guardedly.

"Cholera!" Mama gasped.

"Don't worry, Maria," he comforted Mama. "I can take care of it."

Ghulam started giving orders, "Get me a raw egg, a little bit of wormwood, and a few young leaves of willow." We had plenty of these trees and weeds. Then he added, "Bring me a small bowl, a teaspoon, and a small sharp knife."

The word knife made me shudder.

Everyone dispersed into different direction to fetch the ingredients for the "medicine."

When all the ingredients arrived, he reached into his pocket and produced a handkerchief tied in a knot. He ceremoniously untied the knot and revealed a small dark-brown waxy-looking object resembling a small glob of tree resin—opium. I started shivering.

Ghulam cut a tiny bit of opium, and to it he added a bit of willow leaf and the same amount of wormwood. He mixed them in the bowl, and crushed them with the spoon. Then he cracked the egg, separated the yolk from the white, poured a small portion of the yolk into the bowl, and ceremoniously mixed them.

Onlookers watched Ghulam's moves with heightened curiosity. After mixing the elixir, he carefully scooped the contents into the teaspoon, and said, "Open your mouth."

I stared at Mama. She said, "Open your mouth, son." I did. Quick like lightning, Ghulam emptied the contents into my mouth, pinched my nose and shut my mouth with his hand, and firmly said, "Swallow!"

The concoction was so bitter I almost passed out. The medicine was worse than the cholera. I should have swallowed the darned thing right away, but I couldn't flush it down. My gullet was paralyzed. The longer I swished it in my mouth, trying to get rid of the terrible thing, the worse I felt. I don't know how, but I managed to force it down.

Someone carried me into the house, put me to bed, and made me comfortable.

The warm down comforter felt pleasant. Eventually, my cramps subsided. Then followed hallucinations and nightmares. At first, I felt as if I was a huge checkerboard: the black-and-white of the board kept flashing like neon lights with changing rapidity and color.

Then I was transformed into a spiral. I would spin out with terrifying speed, increasing in size so that I covered the sky. The spinning would stop. Then the whirling would start in reverse direction, and I would be squeezed into a minute microbe. Then the checkerboard and the spiral would compete, tormenting me.

I don't know how long I was tortured, but I woke up in sweat and was totally spent. The cramps were completely gone. Apparently, while I propelled through space, Ghulam gave additional instruction for treating me.

In the evening, Mama gave me a little chicken broth. And before bedtime, she brought a five-gallon tin can container, and poured very hot water into it. She added nettles, wormwood weeds, and willow branches. She forced my legs into the almost scalding water, covered my head with a blanket and made me breathe the hot vapor. This therapy continued twice a day for three, four days until I felt strong enough to have regular meals.

Strange thing, these hallucinations occasionally returned several years later. The last time these nightmares attacked me was when I reached my twenty-first birthday.

Once I related my encounter with cholera to a physician and asked him if there was any value with all those "medications." He explained that the opium served as a relaxant, the egg yolk—as nourishment to give strength, the willow served as a pain reliever, like an aspirin. As for the wormwood—he had no idea.

God sends gift of healing even to humble cattle herders like Ghulam.

Chapter 39

When I Disobeyed Mama

I was born in a caul, or cowl, meaning a child born with a membrane covering its head and face. It's a rare occurrence; it happens once in 80,000 births. Russians call it "born in a shirt." One born in a caul was considered born with good fortune. My grandfather told my mother that I was destined to be a spiritual leader in the family.

Mama took this prediction to heart and put forth her best effort to raise me to be the person her father-in-law prophesied. She taught me to recite some Biblical passages by heart, like the Lord's prayer, Psalm 23, "The Lord is my shepherd"; Psalm 90, "Lord You have been our dwelling place in all generations"; Psalm 91, "He who dwells in the secret place of the Most High"; Psalm 121," I will lift up my eye to the hills."

These four Psalms I had to memorize in their entirety, plus other passages from the Bible, including the Ten Commandments. On occasion, when we had family worship, Mama always asked me to pray, which included recitation of appropriate passages from the Bible.

The seventh day Sabbath, Saturday, was the most sacred time of the week. She raised me with the Fear of God. However, she never threatened me with the horrors of hell. In fact, she never talked to me about hell. To her, salvation was keeping the law.

It was not until later in her life that she learned about, and accepted, salvation by grace. At this point, salvation included grace and law. She did not distinguish between doing God's will and keeping God's law. They were the same. Mama's other virtues were honesty, obedience, truth, and clean language.

She inculcated these virtues into my mind since childhood. She used to say, "Son, don't do bad things. If I catch you doing a bad thing, first I'll warn you never to do it again, but if you do it, I'll punish you severely." And punishment she dispensed freely, applying Solomon's rod generously. Strange thing, with a couple of exceptions, I always told Mama the truth, but not always to those I did not respect—as if they weren't worthy to hear pure truth.

One time, when I was fifteen, my sister Nadya became pregnant with her first child, and because the Gorbenkos lived far from the village, in the forest with their apiary, she was brought to live with us. Birthing was successful. The child, a girl, was named Galina in honor of Paul's younger sister who was left behind in the Ukraine, when the father and his two sons escaped to Iran. A few days after birth Galya, short for Galina, became seriously sick. Her whole body was covered with dandruff-like scales, and it appeared as if she was about to expire her last breath.

Mama summoned me, gave me the famous copper cup (the one with which Nastya put out the fire with milk), and asked me to put water into it and recite Psalm 91 over the water to anoint the dying child with the "holy" water.

I was in shock.

I felt that I, a teenager, was asked to do a "prophet's" job! I refused. Nadya was weeping.

"How can you refuse, when the child is dying and you're refusing to do your job?!" Mama spoke in the firmest tone of voice.

"I don't believe in this," I retorted.

Then, in desperation, she uttered some dreadful words that haunted me most of my life. "If the child dies, it will be on your head!"

Those words struck me like a thunderbolt. I grabbed the cup, poured some water into it, and ran into the barn. I hid in the darkest corner of the barn, away from any eyes and the sound of wailing, and poured my heart out with fear and hatred.

I pleaded, "God, I'm forced to do something I don't believe in. I don't want to be responsible for the girl's death. I'll say the prayer over the water anyway. Heal the child!" It was not a request. There was no "if Your will be done." It was a command.

This was the first time when I addressed God directly and personally, without simple rote recitation of passages from the Bible. I recited the Psalm 91 because I was ordered to. To this day many Russians believe that this Psalm has some magic about it.

I ran back into the house, almost spilling the "holy" water, shoved the cup into Mama's hand, and ran back to my private hiding spot in the barn.

Galya revived.

I did not expect gratitude. I expected thrashing for balking during a critical moment. Obedience is not rewarded with gratitude. Obedience is not a favor—it's a responsibility.

For many years, as Galya grew, I carried a heavy burden, thinking that I forced the Almighty to do something that was not His will. I thought of Hezekiah, King of Judah, when God told him that he should bring his kingdom in order because he would not survive his terminal ailment. The king pleaded with God to extend his life. God granted his prayer and added fifteen years to his life. During those fifteen years, Hezekiah displeased God and was punished for it. During the extended time, the king had a son, named Manasseh, who turned out to be a wicked king, leading his subjects into terrible sin. I was afraid that the same history would repeat here.

It did not.

Part IX

Chapter 40

Under Soviet Occupation

It was August of 1941, when for the first time in our lives, we heard the sound of an airplane. We even saw one or two of them, high in the eastern sky. Later, a single plane flew over our village, dropping a shower of leaflets, which descended like faded birds with broken wings. We scrambled to catch some in the air.

The message on these leaflets was in Farsi, of course, none of us could read Farsi at that time. Later, we found out that the message was friendly, that we should not fear of anything. However, many people from Persian villages were running towards the mountains in fear.

After all, their country was being invaded, and an enemy spells trouble. The road to the mountains led through Rahmatabad, and these villagers hurried through our village on foot with their chattel, on donkeys, and on carts. They ignored the friendly messages from the sky as they could not read them.

One day as we worked in the vegetable garden, a small, one-engine plane flew so low over our heads that we could see people waving to us from the plane. We waved back. We were sure the plane was Russian because of a red star on each wing. Whoever they were, I'm sure they recognized that ours was a Russian village. The huts in Persian villages huddled in groups, while the Russian ones stretched along a single street, with homes on either side of it and vegetable gardens in the back.

Shortly thereafter, Soviet military personnel appeared in Rahmatabad in a military vehicle—a complete surprise. We didn't know what to expect, joy or fear. Should we welcome them with bread and salt or run away from them?

Our fears were assuaged, when the uniformed men greeted us with friendly smiles. We surrounded them with excitement. Some village men were vying for the privilege of hosting these visitors in their homes. The lucky person who got the honor was Vasiliy Ivanovich Muravyov, the *katkhudo* at the time.

In Prokhladnoye, the village elders discouraged young people from socializing with the worldly military personnel. Now that they were cut off from their homeland for several years, they welcomed these soldiers warmly.

These few Red Army soldiers were the harbingers of the hordes of them visiting our homes.

One evening, a whole convoy of trucks roared into our village with loads of soldiers and parked their trucks along our only street.

Only a few of them, probably the officers, left the truck and visited with villagers. The rest stayed atop the trucks sitting on boards stretched across. Curious, I inspected a few trucks, listening to their private conversation.

To my great surprise, I heard a female voice, and decided to linger longer at this truck. The woman soldier was talking about her life back at home. I remember I felt sorry for her. Here she was far away from home, among all those male soldiers without any company of her own gender.

Some soldiers made regular visitations to our village. Here they were, away from their homes, in a foreign country with strange culture and being treated as enemies. In our village they found an oasis, where they were welcomed with open arms and treated like favorite sons. Here they could find some peace from barracks and the nagging worry about being deployed to the front lines.

They were only some 30 miles away in Gorgon, where they were stationed. No wonder, our village attracted them. Here they could spend their free time in peaceful surroundings. Dare I say that in our community they felt more at peace than even at their own homes?

Here, people lived in self-exile, isolated, fenced off from fear of dreadful world events. There was no sound of whistling bullets, no roar of tanks nor explosion of bombs. And, most of all, no KGB (Soviet intelligence agency) agents with straining ears.

Here people spoke publicly what was on their mind. They could profess any faith they wished without reprisals from religious or government entities. Our young men were immune from the fear of military draft. And when our young people married, they had no fear of forced separation.

So, when these military men from our previous world appeared on our doorsteps, we wanted to know what was happening back in our previous homeland. Even though these soldiers basked in our peaceful environment, they still could not relax and speak their mind. They could not satisfy all our curiosities.

Some groups preferred to visit one family, and some another. Soon we became bonded with one group that visited us frequently. They began to ask us about our past, and we of their lives.

In Russian culture at that time, smoking inside a house was considered bad manners. So, when someone needed a drag of nicotine, he stepped outside.

One evening, after we had told them of our escape from Russia, one soldier by the name of Peter, on the pretense of needing to smoke, stepped outside. My brother Mikhail followed him. This is what my brother told us after the soldiers left.

Peter had served in the military outpost on the Iranian-Soviet border near Prokhladnoye when we escaped. He remembered that event. The Soviet guards were ordered to intercept a large contraband. While they were about to return to their outpost, one of the two men who were left to guard their post, galloped with troubling news—all the villagers had disappeared.

The commander of the outpost ordered his outfit to pursue the escapees. By the time they reached the border, it was too late. The fugitives were already safe on the other side of the border.

The Soviets were not going to give up the pursuit that easily. They approached the Persian border guards for negotiations to return the runaways. Between a good-sized bribe from the Soviets, and the khan's fury who breathed revenge, the deal was easily accomplished.

Peter went on to say that Soviet guards were to set an ambush on the Soviet-Iranian border, and the Persian guards were to force us to move towards the trap at night. He said that they had waited for us the whole night, but before dawn, when we didn't show up, the Persian guards hurried toward our encampment.

The Russians, impatient and frustrated, dared to cross the border. They reached the camp, but found no one there. Then, in the early dawn, they saw the last wagon dip beyond the mountain crest.

Peter concluded the story by quoting the commander's words, *"Раз так, Бог с ними."* (If that's the way, God be with them.) Then, he raised his hand and commanded, *"А теперь, братцы, живо домой!"* (And now, fellows, hurry home!)

God moves in mysterious ways. In our case, He previously had sent us a redeemer in the form of a humble shepherd.

We bonded with this group of soldiers. In fact, so much so, that my sister Tatiana (Tanya) had a crush on Peter. And he was not indifferent to her.

Occasionally, they came with some presents. One time they came with their own vodka and smoked fish. Of course, none of us drank any liquor. After they had departed, they left their smoked fish on the table.

While Mama and my brothers went outside to say goodbye to them, my sisters and I tried the fish. It was delicious beyond words. Then Mama walked in. When she saw us gorging ourselves on fish, she shouted, "Don't eat that stuff, it's unclean." I was so disappointed that I'd wished I'd eaten faster.

One time they brought us a sealed five-gallon can of American flour and presented it to Nastya, my sister-in-law. Nastya was a master in baking delicious bread. When she baked the bread from American white flour, it turned out to be a piece of art—fit for a tsar. The white bread rose so high, and so beautifully, that we hated to cut it. We wanted to enjoy just looking at it with admiration.

One wet November evening (the soldiers always came in the evening), they appeared at our door. My brother, Aleksey, an exceptionally hospitable host, sent me to David Popov's home at the other end of the village to obtain two bottles of vodka made from fermented raisins.

Such brewing was always kept a secret, but somehow, everyone knew where it was brewed. I was glad to comply—anything for our special guests. Though the rain had stopped, the street was muddy with puddles and I had to negotiate around, hopping over them. The evening was cold but bright, because the moon was almost full, and moonshine shone through the clouds.

After teasing me, Uncle David (we always called all adults "uncles" and "aunts") gave me two bottles of his secret brew. Always a curious kid, I wondered what was so peculiar about vodka that everyone loved.

I decided to find out.

I uncorked the bottle with my teeth and took a gulp. The liquid was so bitter and powerful, it hit me in the nose. Instead of spitting it out, I forced it down my throat anyway. It felt like fire hissing down my throat. Then I began to worry—one bottle was full, the other had a bit of empty space.

Instead of spilling on the mud to make the contents even, I gulped the firewater from the other full bottle, and started plodding along. Soon I felt very warm and unsteady on my feet. In fact, I couldn't negotiate the puddles successfully. Then, I mumbled, "Who cares?" In fact, stomping through the puddles was fun.

Despite the chilly night, I arrived home sweaty and muddy. I gave the bottles to Aleksey and complained about the muddy street. If anyone noticed my imbalance, no one said a word about it.

I did find out what the moonshine tasted like, but I still couldn't figure out what fun people found in that choking, horrid-tasting stuff.

After a while, our new comrades had stopped their visits to us for a few months. We missed them very much, especially Peter.

One evening, they returned, looking tired and gaunt—minus Peter. When we inquired of his absence, they sadly informed us that he had been killed in a battle. They did not go into the details of Peter's death. Our joy of seeing them turned into sadness. Tanya left the room. That ended the budding pointless romance.

Somehow, these young soldiers felt quite at home in our village. They brought us records of old and new Russian folk songs. Every other week, they brought us movies, which, at first, they showed on a white sheet, spread on the wall of a hut or stretched between two posts outdoors, weather permitting. Later, they arrived with a portable movie van. They showed the movies through a tube-like screen that extended from the side of the van like a huge accordion. Some of those movies were classics, which went on to enter worldwide archives, and, occasionally, are shown on TV to this day.

The subject matter of these movies was historical, glorifying Soviet military power, skill of fighting on the battlefield, and, especially, patriotism for communism. I remember one scene, where a partisan, before tossing a long-handled grenade and kissing it, shouted, *"За родину! За Сталина!"* (For homeland! For Stalin!) He then hurtled it at the Germans.

Though these movies brought entertainment, they also produced tremendous effect in viewers, especially on the children. After viewing these films, the following day children played war, and each one of them wanted to be a Communist hero.

They also influenced the young adults. Some boys began to experiment with homemade cigarettes and vodka—moonshine brewing increased. A few older parents tried to prevent their children from attending the outdoor "theater." However, spiritual training was no match for such powerful attraction as Soviet propaganda films.

Some young adults, and even a couple of families, returned to Russia from Iran at the end of WWII. How they were accepted by the Communists, and how they fared in the "homeland," I personally do not know much.

The story went something like this: These youths were to write letters to their relatives back in Iran and send some photographs. They also agreed that if life were good in the Soviet Union, they would pose in a standing position in photographs. If not, then in seating position. Supposedly, they did send some pictures of themselves—in lying position with sad faces. I hadn't seen such pictures or had known one who had received them—just talk.

During Gorbachev's glasnost (meaning "openness" as in political or governmental transparency), one of my classmates, Lyudmila Titova, attended a Seventh-day Adventist evangelistic meeting in Moscow and became acquainted with the evangelist, who later invited her to America to visit her relatives. I had the privilege of meeting her at our house in California. We didn't talk much about personal life.

Then in 1997, I met Lyudmila in Moscow, in the Adventist Euro-Asian Division Headquarters, where we had a long time, one-on-one occasion. She did say that shortly after their return to Russia, life was very hard for them. After all, WWII had just ended, and the Soviet Union had to bind its wounds and put its life back in order.

Later, when the Soviet government discovered that Lyudmila had a good command of the Farsi (Persian) and Russian languages, they used her as a radio announcer in Farsi, beaming their "news" to the Iranian citizens.

It seemed to me her only joy in life was the memory of her past, her happy, carefree young life in an American boarding academy. Even in her late sixties, her hairstyle hadn't changed since she was sixteen. The topic of our conversation centered on our former classmates.

She said she had been married and had two boys. Both of her parents had passed away. I told her I had a crush on her, but because of her intelligence and her cultured background, and because of my peasantry, I didn't dare let her know of my feelings toward her. When I told her that to me she was a princess, she was pleased to hear it.

She asked me to put it in writing. I did, and always addressed her as a princess in all my letters to her. I wanted to see her apartment, but she declined the request. She said her apartment was not in proper order for guests. She also did not talk about her own personal life, or that of her parents.

For several years after our meeting in Moscow, we exchanged all the pictures we had of our boarding school years. For reasons unknown to me, we lost contact with one other. I called her on several occasions, but couldn't get through. That was the end of our contact.

Chapter 41

Yashka's Jackals

During WWII, the Soviet military still employed some outdated forms of warfare, like cavalry. The Red Army kept horses in Gorgon. Wherever there are horses, horse feed is essential. So it was with the Soviet cavalry.

My oldest brother Aleksey had heard that Soviet soldiers needed hay for their horses. To supplement our income, he decided to do some haying. One late spring, he dragged me along to help him with the job. I was about thirteen years old.

Most of our villagers were farmers, and in our culture, only manual labor was considered a noble vocation. A desk job was for lazy and crooked people. My oldest brother, Aleksey, leaned toward the latter point of view. Conversely, my oldest sister, Margarita, and I, both preferred books to plows. Because of our preferences for mental labor, we were looked upon with mild disdain for our aversion to farming; although, few did look up to us for our desire for education.

Here, I must admit, I hated farming in every form. I would rather attend school, do homework or read the Bible, than do farm chores like cleaning the barn or plowing a field.

Aleksey was just the opposite. He loved farming and tending to animals, especially the horses. He treated the equine as if they were his children. Subsequently, we were not the best of friends.

One early Sunday morning in springtime, Aleksey and I loaded our wagon with provisions—scythes, rakes, and pitchforks—and headed towards lush fields not far from Gorgon, for a whole week. We arrived at our destination late one afternoon.

"Yasha, take the horses into the field and hobble them so they can graze," said Aleksey. "Oh, also put things in order and fix supper, while I start cutting hay." Chores assigned, Aleksey put a scythe over his shoulder and headed for the green fields.

I hobbled the horses as asked, then removed their bridles and brought them to camp, hanging them up on their post. As far as bringing camp to order, it took me forever, placing things in wrong places.

When it came to cooking, I knew exactly what to do. In no time, I had a cooking fire blazing. In a cast-iron skillet, chicken sizzled in sesame oil with some herbs. Rice steeped in a small cauldron.

At sundown, Aleksey returned. He had checked things at camp and was upset. "What a mess you created here. I can't find a thing. Can't you do simple things right?"

"I tried," I mumbled, avoiding Aleksey's angry glare.

"Trying's not good enough. What you need is a good thrashing."

I felt as if some animals began gnawing at my stomach.

"Let's have supper, now. I'm starving," said Aleksey in a softer tone. The moment Aleksey bit off a mouthful of fried chicken, he released a sigh of satisfaction. Then, through a chicken-filled mouth he added in a conciliatory tone, "You may be clumsy in everything else, but you do cook delicious food."

His compliment pacified the inner animals inside of me.

"Now, go after the horses and bring them to camp."

"Sure," said I, happy he liked the meal. I cheerfully ran to fetch the bridles from the post upon which I hung them, out of reach of the jackals.

Now, jackals will devour anything made of animal product, including raw hide. They have a keen sense of smell. Not a thing, if insecurely stored, can escape their sharp teeth. Harnesses, and even our homemade rawhide shoes, had to be hung up high on posts or hidden under pillows. Otherwise, jackals would devour them for dessert.

When I reached for the bridles, I was shocked to find only one there. Frantically, I searched for the other one, but it was nowhere to be found. I must have dropped it after I put the horses out to pasture.

"What am I going to do? What am I going to do?" I muttered to myself, stomping my foot.

It wasn't what Aleksey would say or do to me that bothered me. It was my own inattentiveness I could not forgive. At that moment, I would gladly have preferred Aleksey's thrashing if only that would correct the situation. The gnawing animals inside my guts were, again, awakened.

"How could I be so absentminded?" I shouted into the night. There was nothing else left to do but go after the horses. I gripped the one bridle, grabbed a rope, and tried to retrace my steps, hoping to find the bridle. No such luck.

I found the horses and put the bridle on one. Then, I improvised a bridle out of the rope and put it on the other horse, and brought them back to camp.

Just as I lay down to sleep, I heard a prolonged plaintive howl of a lone jackal. Another jackal answered the solo howl, then another and another. Soon packs of them surrounded the camp, howling as if they were trying to outdo each other. It sounded as if they were mocking me, mimicking my anguished moan. I imagined the jackals feasting over the lost bridle. This time, the "animals" inside me were really tearing me apart. I writhed in agony, but nothing helped.

How can I face Aleksey? I thought. *How can we hitch the horses to the wagon without the bridle? Why am I so stupid?*

Then a new thought occurred to me. *How about a prayer? Impossible. God does not help stupid people. I don't deserve a miracle.* Then I remembered the story of Daniel in the lions' den.

If God answered Daniel's prayer and made them act like kittens, I thought, *perhaps He can help me, too.*

"No. God would not help me with my stupidity," I mumbled.

Another thought dawned on me. Jesus had promised, "Whatsoever you shall ask in My name, that will I do." The more I dwelled on this thought the more I took courage to pray. And pray I did, as never before. In my prayer, I asked God to keep the jackals away from the bridle and to direct me to the lost bridle. Then, I added, "Not because I want to avoid the beating in the morning. I deserve that, but because we won't be able to do our work tomorrow."

In no time, the jackals inside me calmed down a bit, and I fell asleep.

"Yasha, wake up," Aleksey called in the morning. "Take the horses into pasture and hobble them, then come back and fix breakfast."

By now my mind had cleared, and I remembered the bridle and my prayer. The jackals in the pit of my stomach awoke, too—but not to the severity of the night before.

Without saying a word to Aleksey, I took the one bridle and rope off the post and led the horses to the same spot where I had taken them the evening before, retracing my steps. Now, it was not my jackals that tortured me, it was the vacillation between hope and doubt.

I hobbled the horses and headed back, again retracing my steps, repeating the words and pleading, "Lord, help. Lord, please lead me to the bridle."

As I dragged my feet through dewy grass, I stumbled over something. The lost bridle! All wet and slimy.

I was so overwhelmed at the thought that God would answer *my* prayer that I started laughing and crying at the same time. I wanted to thank God, but a simple "thank you" wasn't good enough, so I continued to laugh through tears. I picked up the precious present, dried it on my pants, and hopped and skipped all the way to camp. Best of all, the gnawing inside me immediately stopped, and self-respect returned.

Chapter 42

Beyond Dreams

One day, when I reached my sixteenth birthday, our church elder, Aleksey Ivanovich Muravyov, received a letter from the Seventh-day Adventist Conference in Teheran, Iran's capital. Since no one else could read Farsi, Aleksey called me.

Though the message was written in a business language, beyond my ability to comprehend the whole message, I was able to decipher that the American Adventist missionaries were opening a school in Teheran and were looking for candidates to attend this school. My first reaction was confusion. "What's that got to do with us?"

Then suddenly, my mind went berserk. I felt an influx of hot flashes. I was on fire. This was an opportunity beyond my dreams! Me, poor barefooted peasant attending an American school in the Capital? Impossible! It was simply beyond any dream. It was like someone inviting me to go to another planet. I read the letter several times over to become convinced of the veracity of the message. I was afraid I was wrong. Aleksey Ivanovich, too, didn't quite believe me. He took the letter to the village schoolteacher for confirmation. The teacher confirmed my guess.

Aleksey kept the letter until Sabbath, when the Adventists returned from their fields to worship God. After church service, according to our custom, when all the church members assembled at some family's house for Sabbath dinner and singing, Aleksey Muravyov mentioned the news from the Conference. He added that the Conference was planning a boarding school in the capital and is looking for students. No one paid any attention about the school; it was something otherworldly—something for the rich people in a faraway world. Besides, they said, there were no such candidates in our church for such a school.

"No," responded my eldest brother Aleksey. "I'm sure it's not free. Who's going to pay for such an education?" That was the end of the conversation about my future.

Mama said nothing. However, deep down in her heart she had yearned for a decent education acquired by anyone among her children.

Elder Muravyov said, "How about Yashka? He's a good student. He would make an excellent candidate."

A few weeks after receiving the letter about a school in the capital, the president of the Adventist Conference with his family, and Elder Beitzakhar, visited our congregation in an unmarked American ambulance, purchased from the US Army returning home from WWII.

At Sabbath dinner, the president mentioned the school in Teheran, and asked if we had any candidates for it. There ensued a corporate silence. Everyone gazed at my family.

My brother, Aleksey, said sheepishly, "We don't have such a person."

"How about your brother Yakov?" asked Mikhail Semyonovich.

"Yes, how about him?' added Aleksey Muravyov.

"What do you think about it, Maria Sevastyanovna?" asked Elder Beitzakhar.

She thought a moment and then slowly responded, "It's possible." Then, taking a deep breath, she added, "There is one big question, we have no money to pay for my son's education."

Elder Beitzakhar translated this conversation to Elder Crider, the Conference president. When the question about the money arose, Elder Crider asked Mama, "How do you pay for things you buy at the store?"

My brother Aleksey joined the conversation, "We sell flour to buy these things."

The president quickly responded, "This is a boarding school, and the school will need flour. Could you somehow pay with flour?"

"It's possible, but we need our brother on the farm," Aleksey protested weakly.

"No problem," responded Mama, "I'll work in his place."

The deal was made. Mom always had the last word.

When I heard the news that I would be studying in a boarding school in the Capital—in an American school—I could not feel the ground under my feet! That night I could not sleep. Neither the Sandman nor Orpheus could calm me down. Somehow, toward the morning, Nature took over, and I fell asleep.

The departure was to take place after Sabbath. That Friday, the preparation day, I did all my chores in haste, as if to shorten time. I attacked my chores with vengeance, saying farewell to all my responsibilities, and I even patted the horses, as if saying good-bye to them. The adrenaline kept pumping energy.

Sabbath day was the same. I knew it was a last Sabbath, and I felt special. My mind was spinning all over the world. I don't remember the sermon, but I certainly remember what happened after the church service. Aleksey Ivanovich Muravyov, who functioned as our Elder, took me aside and addressed me formally as an adult.

He spoke slowly and deliberately in his peasant speech, "Yakov Isayevich, you are a very special person, and we all love you. We expect much out of you. You are going to an American school in Teheran to get education. Study very hard. Learn everything you can. When you learn everything, come back, and I promise we will build you a new school and a new church. You will teach our children some learning, and us, the Word of God."

At first, I didn't pay much attention to this injunction. My mind was reeling with excitement and anticipation of getting out of the village into the big world. The powerful impact of this exhortation hit me later.

The day of farewell from Rahmatabad arrived. It was 1946. After a painfully long breakfast, Elders Crider and Beitzakhar finally rolled their ambulance to our house and loaded five 100-lb sacks of flour into the vehicle—my annual tuition for boarding school.

Mama had already tied my possessions in a bundle, a change of homemade clothes. One final custom had to be performed. All entered our house, formed a circle around me, and I knelt for the blessing. Mama asked Mikhail Beitzakhar to say a prayer. After prayer, family members hugged and kissed me.

Mama was the last person to hug me with crushing embrace, and in a shaky voice said, "God bless you, my son. Study hard and don't give up. I'll pray for you." Then she took a paper currency out of her pocket and handed it to me. It was all the money she had in her possession—one dollar. I felt as if she was tearing a part of her heart and giving it to me. I saw tears in her eyes.

I had never seen Mama crying, not even at Batya's funeral, but on this occasion, she wiped her tears. Seeing those tears crushed me—I wanted to cry. I didn't know, I still don't, whether she cried because she was going to miss me, or because her lifetime dream had finally become reality.

One of her children would get the education that she never had.

Part X

Chapter 43

Facing a New World

Finally, we climbed into the ambulance. The engine roared. We started moving slowly at first. I stared back through the rear window and saw my family huddled together, waving.

Mama raised her apron up to her eyes. Then the reality hit me—*I may never see them again.* I felt I was torn away from my family. Deep down in my guts, I felt like getting off the ambulance. As the vehicle gained speed, my family grew smaller and smaller, until they totally disappeared in the dust behind.

When you grow up in one environment, and especially, when you reach teenage years, home becomes boring and stifling. Then comes a period when you itch for some radical change in your life; you crave adventure, independence from parental pressure.

In your inner heart, your parents seem old-fashioned. Parents don't realize that the world is changing, but they pressure you to conform to their dying world. Your ship of destiny is about to sail off to some glorious future, but you feel shackled to your slow-witted parents.

Their love, that once warmed you, now burns you. You want to run away somewhere where you want to be yourself, free, not accountable to anyone.

Then, "miraculously," you find yourself on your ship, at last. You exhale a heavy sigh of relief. You feel free. Free. Free! You toss your shackles overboard and do what you dreamed of doing. You plunge into this life of freedom with abandonment. You stuff your mouth with rich pastry until you're surfeited to the gills.

Then your ship begins to rock on ocean waves. The waves increase with intensity. Before you realize it, your ship is in the middle of a squall. Your delicious rum cake ends up on your lap. Perhaps you begin to think of your Mama.

My sudden abandonment, of my previous life, was not quite as dramatic as I have just painted for you. I loved my family, loved the mountains, the forest, and freedom of space, but I loved education more.

Besides, Mama was happy for this opportunity that had come my way. She rejoiced. I hadn't realized at the time that all these impossibilities became possible through Providence above. At sixteen, these adventures appearing to a teenager was a mere lark.

Although the distance from Rahmatabad to Tehran is some 270 miles, the trip was an arduous expedition. Traveling along a two-lane gravel road, over the crest of the Elburz Mountain Range, following slow trucks up steep inclines, pushing through herds of cattle, sheep, and donkeys—all take a toll on the driver's and the passengers' nerves.

Even though I had traveled through these mountains some years back, it was by train and at night. Now, these sights at daytime fascinated me; the shores of the Caspian, rivers, rocky cliffs, gorges and the bridges over them.

This eye-opening yet nerve-wracking trek took a whole day. We arrived at the Adventist Mission Compound late at night. To say we were exhausted would be an understatement, especially for the sole driver, Elder Crider.

Since it was a late, hot summer day, we were lodged on top of the flat roof of the Mission building. My emotions were on overload. I couldn't sleep for some time as the roar of the ambulance engine resonated in my ears. Besides, I was fascinated with all the electric lights around me. I had never seen such brightness at night. Eventually, nature took over and my nerves calmed.

In the morning, Elder Beitzakhar asked me why I kept yelling, periodically, in my sleep, getting up and walking while still yelling. He took me for a lunatic. He had to grab me, wake me up and send me back to sleep.

It finally dawned on me—I was dreaming I was in the watermelon patch keeping the critters away. Good thing I didn't walk off the three-story roof and crash among some rose bushes. Worse yet, I could've mistaken Elder Beitzakhar for a bear and attack him. I would certainly have ended up in some psychic asylum, instead of a boarding academy.

For an ignorant sixteen-year-old peasant boy, suddenly finding himself in an American Conference President's home, in a capital city, no less, was challenging—an understatement. I might as well have been on a different planet.

Some things in this new culture shocked me: like saying grace before a meal while seated, eating my breakfast with a fork, getting used to strange food, being terrified by an overflowing flushed toilet.

I experienced fear, bewilderment, embarrassment, and, most of all, fascination. I felt like a strayed wild animal in a large city—noise, traffic, paved streets, cameras flashing. Every day, new experiences barraged me. Thankfully, Elder

Beitzakhar took me to his home before school started. There I felt a little bit relaxed.

When World War II ended, the Seventh-day Adventist Headquarters in America determined to take opportunity of somewhat relaxed relations with the Soviets, and send some missionaries to Soviet Union. Church leaders sent few young couples to college for a crash course in Russian language. After the war, they ended up in Tehran, waiting for entrance visas for passage into communist country. When missionaries applied for entrance visas into the USSR, the Soviet embassy refused to issue them.

After all, the Soviets were desperately eradicating local religions in their country, let alone accepting foreign ones. Secondly, the Soviet Union was in ruins after a devastating war, and the country needed manpower to bring it back to its normal state. Foreigners were a liability to them. Young American missionaries were stranded in Tehran.

The Adventist denomination dispersed these missionaries throughout the Middle East. One family chose to found a boarding academy in Iran.

It was 1946. The countries of Britain, USA, and the Soviet Union were involved in liberating Iran from their occupation thereof. The United States had the most military hardware.

Americans were not about to haul their possessions back home across oceans. It would be like taking firewood into the forest. Consequently, they decided to sell their leftovers dirt cheap to whoever wanted it. The Soviet Union acquired thousands upon thousands of military vehicles.

Americans offered Iran military uniforms for almost nothing. Iranian officials arrogantly refused to buy American "rags." The former took the refusal for an offense and said, "You don't want to pay for rags, you'll get rags for free."

So, they organized brigades of GIs with scissors to open bales of brand new uniforms and cut them up in various places. Then, they dumped this American, taxpayer property onto the Iranian Red Cross grounds. Some Iranian entrepreneurs purchased this slightly damaged property from the Red Cross and made big money on it. And some of these American uniforms even reached Rahmatabad.

The Adventists were not about to lose an opportunity to acquire much needed materials for a fledgling boarding school. They purchased an ambulance, a truck, a Jeep, bedding, cafeteria items and kitchenware, a piano, and barrels of preserved food products. Naturally, all these possessions were to be transported to the school site.

The missionaries rented three houses in a mountainous picturesque resort, a few blocks away from the Shah's summer palace. One spacious house was designated for classrooms, a neighboring one for the boys' dormitory and religious gatherings. A third house, a few buildings up the hill, was designated for the principal's residence and a girls' dormitory.

The principal's family consisted of four member, Paul and Ruth Boynton with their two children, Sue Ann and Paul Jr., also headed for the boarding house.

They named the academy Iran Training School (ITS).

Chapter 44

Preparing the Academy for Classes

Since I had nothing to do, I was inducted to help ready ITS for classes about to begin. I was informed to pack my meager possessions, wait for transportation.

The day had arrived. On Sunday morning, Anastasia Semyonovna, Elder Beitz's wife, fixed me breakfast; feta cheese and halva, rolled in soft lavash, something like a middle-eastern pocket bread, and hot tea.

Before long, I heard the beep of a Jeep. I thanked the host for breakfast and for the family's hospitality, and raced down the stairs from the second floor.

At the entrance to the apartment complex awaited the Jeep, with a young driver and two Armenian boys my age. I said *Salaam* to the strangers in the vehicle and positioned myself behind the dark-haired driver, with my possessions in my lap.

We all waved to Anastasia, and the Jeep took off. Cool morning breezes blew into my face. I had never been in a topless vehicle before—except wagons with galloping horses in the country. The wind in my face, and the novelty of being in an American military automobile, energized me and made me feel important. I wished my Rahmatabad friends could see me.

Our driver wove through Tehran traffic, his hair flying, as he constantly beeped the horn. We boys hung on to our caps. The two boys spoke cheerfully to each other in Armenian. I was ignored. But I was thoroughly enjoying myself in this new excitement in my life, observing the unobstructed sights. New-to-me Iranian city smells fascinated me.

Now we were climbing up to Shemiran, a region along the Elburz Range. The Jeep roared. I was amazed at the ease with which this brown vehicle gained elevation. My ears popped.

We finally reached our destination, the spacious graveled ground of the boys' dormitory. The Jeep crunched around the swimming pool (most Iranian residences have some sort of pool), and stopped near a truck which was loaded to the brim with American military mattresses. A few feet ahead stood a small building, perhaps for the owner's servants quarters, now empty.

It was already early afternoon. The hired cook served us lunch with a lot of greens: bitter arugula, tarragon, basil, and romaine lettuce, all uncut. We ate them with our fingers, sometimes wrapped into a bread pocket with Feta cheese; the lettuce—we dipped into flavored, sweet liquid and simply crunched.

After lunch, we were to haul the mattresses into the servants' quarters. Besides the three of us, there were about a half dozen other Armenian boys, some older. We stacked the mattresses almost to the ceiling. With all the bedding in place and no more chores for the time being, a few boys decided to have a wrestling match, one of Persians' favorite sports. Some aggressive older boys challenged everyone to show their prowess in this sport.

A boy named Mishik with black curly hair, son of a former wrestler, challenged me. He was talented and often participated in school activities, like singing during religious services. He had already learned and spoke some English, and appeared to be a favorite among the adults. His father had, at the time, a small successful tailor shop, and a couple of employees. The father was highly respected in the church and in the community.

Once before, Mishik had visited Rahmatabad and challenged my friend, Ivan, and me to a wrestling match. I had declined. I was no wrestler, and I knew it. But Ivan had accepted the challenge, and before he knew it, he was flat on his back. Mishik stood over Ivan triumphantly. I remembered that clearly. And now at ITS, Mishik challenged all the boys to wrestle with him. Once again, I refused. While the boys were having fun wrestling, I sat on top of the mattresses observing the noisy, grunting commotion. Soon, I was bored and left the arena.

Chapter 45

Facing a New Reality

A couple of days later, after morning worship, the boys' dean, Mr. Purhodi, detained me in our "chapel" after services. He said something that shocked and devastated me to my core.

"Jacob, did you take a wallet that was lying on top of the mattresses when the boys were wrestling the other day?" he asked.

"No, I did not," I answered. Stealing was never my vice.

"Who could've taken it then? There was no one else on top of the mattresses beside you." He insisted.

"I don't know. All I know is that I didn't take it," I answered warily.

He interrogated me on "the theft" as if his accusation was an indisputable fact. I felt a tone of impatience in his voice as he pressed on, "Jacob, stealing is a terrible crime. Confess to it. Return the wallet, and everything will be forgotten."

I was taught in childhood to always tell the truth, and it had always been my practice. Everyone believed me. When I claimed I didn't do something, that was enough. End of conversation. Now I faced a new situation: a very important person accusing me of a dreadful crime. I didn't know how to relate to such a thing. I clamped up. I was too stunned to say anything. If someone didn't believe me, what was the point of repeatedly proving my innocence?

A long pause ensued.

"Well? What do you say?" He broke the silence.

I couldn't say anything. Another long silence.

Finally, the dean said, "Okay, you think about it. Pray about it." And he walked out. I sat there wishing I'd stayed in my village, where everyone loved me and believed me. Finally, I climbed up the stairs to the boys' dormitory, entered the common bedroom, and lay on my cot trembling.

Soon, a boy came in and said, "It's time to work." I left my cot, and slowly descended to the first floor and out into the sunny morning. I joined a group of boys, waiting for an assignment. Up until this time, I was ignored; as if I was an outsider, which I was. This time, I felt accusing eyes on me. I preferred being ignored over being stared at. Thankfully, our assignment was to add last touches to the dormitory, Mishik was to help the adults.

It was Thursday, and ITS would be expecting the influx of students.

Thursdays and Fridays were days of noise, laughter, excitement, carrying luggage, opening suitcases, and commotion. Early arrivals brought with them a state of joyful anticipation—except me. I wasn't even interested in any of my Russian friends. A vice-like feeling pressed on my chest. I was an observer rather than a participant, in this youthful, boisterous excitement. I preferred solitude.

Thursday evening, Mrs. Ruth Boynton, the principal's wife, fixed dinner for the few of us who were spending the night on campus. Some of those who lived in the capital preferred spending the night in their homes. Entering Mrs. Boynton's dining room, I was impressed with the bright and cheerful atmosphere. The table was set for a banquet; white tablecloth, bright chinaware, shiny silverware. It was all new to me. I felt both awkward and relieved. I didn't know how to behave. I was relieved because among the guests were two Beitzakhar sisters, Flora and Liza, whom I had already met, and a stranger, Lyudmila Titova, a non-Adventist Russian girl. I watched their dinner manners and tried to imitate them.

Mr. Boynton sat at the head of the table. Guests were seated, dinner was served, and grace was said, but no one started eating until the hostess sat at the table—a new formality to me, a learning experience, indeed.

Mrs. Boynton first poured soup from a soup tureen. Then followed the main course. In the middle of the table sat a bowl with some round and black things. I assumed they were small plums. When someone took a few with a spoon, I took three.

When I put one into my mouth, I was horrified. It was bitter and highly over salted (it happened to be a Greek olive). I didn't dare spit the odious thing, neither could I swallow it. My esophagus was paralyzed. I put some other food into my mouth to minimize the grossness of the object that was choking me. Then, I took a deep breath and one by one forced the rest down my gullet. It was humiliation on top of misery. So much for my enlightenment of things cultural.

The following day, Friday, the rest of the students arrived. It was again a noisy day. Old friends reunited. New acquaintances formed. Even I felt relieved. There were eight Russian-speaking students, a couple Assyrians, and one Iranian. The rest were Armenians from different parts of Iran.

Sabbath morning, Saturday, was a festive celebration. After all, it was the first day of a new boarding academy, in the history of Seventh-day Adventist (SDA) religion, in Iran. Even nature noted this event. The day turned out to be crisp, clear and sunny. Trees displayed a variety of bright colors—yellow, orange, purple, green, vermillion and various shades of red. Campus buzzed with parents and relatives from different parts of Iran, SDA Conference officials, and friends.

All dressed in their finest holiday attire— except me. My best suit was a cotton shirt that my mother sewed lovingly, and cotton beltless, pajama-style pants. I couldn't help but look around at the other boys' garment. Most were dressed in suits and ties. Mishik outshined them all. He was dressed in a tailor-made three-piece suit, starched white shirt and black bowtie. I felt like an albino crow among black ravens. I wanted to hide.

During church service, students sat in the front seats, girls on one side of the "auditorium," boys on the other side. I sat with Russian boys in the last row of chairs. What a contrast! At home I was a favorite, loved, respected, and trusted son. Here, I felt like an outcast.

Without a doubt, this church service surpassed all other church celebrations which I had seen, thus far, in Iran. Singing was boisterous; prayers were touching, speeches impressive. The sermon given by the Conference president, with a translator, was stirring. Students sang gustily, their performance followed by the loudest Amen. Truly, the grand occasion was uplifting and moving. Even nature joined in with the celebrants displaying beauty and breeze.

Ironically, I felt nothing but gloom.

The Sabbath Vespers service was about to begin a bit earlier that day. At least for a while, I was caught up in the festivities of the day. I felt some joy.

Principal Boynton, and Mrs. Boynton, Sue Ann and Paul Jr.

Beitzakhar; 2ⁿᵈ row - 2ⁿᵈ, Mr. Purhodi; 3ʳᵈ and 4ᵗʰ, Mr. & Mrs. Boynton; 3ʳᵈ row and standing - 2ⁿᵈ, Ludmila Titova; 8ᵗʰ, Nadya Shabalina; 4ᵗʰ row and standing - 3ʳᵈ, author; 4ᵗʰ, Evgeniy Grebyonkin; 9ᵗʰ, Gregoriy Gorbenko; 2ⁿᵈ to last, Mishik.

Chapter 46

Bitter Reality

By late afternoon that day, most guests and parents had left "campus." Vespers service was held in the classroom building. Though it was adjacent to the boys' dormitory, it was some fifteen feet higher up on the hill.

Holy Sabbath hours were ending, however, with a painful blow. At the end of Vespers, Mr. Purhodi asked me to follow him outside the building. As we walked over the crunching gravel, the first thing that impressed upon me was the beauty of the gorgeous sunset approaching the horizon below. Its orange hues reflected on a few clouds, enhancing the already colorful, early autumn leaves of fruit trees. But then I felt a crushing alarm. I knew what was coming.

Mr. Purhodi led me to the farthest corner of the yard. He stopped under a tree.

"Wasn't it a beautiful day today?" he asked.

"Yes," I agreed weakly, my heart pounding.

"Jacob, have you thought about the wallet?" Mr. Purhodi came to the point.

After a pause, I angrily stated, "There is nothing to think about. I did not steal the wallet. I did not even see it."

"After this beautiful Sabbath day and the wonderful celebration, you're still denying that you took the wallet?" he insisted pleadingly.

I didn't know what to say any more. I froze again.

The dean resorted to a sermonette. "What you did was a sin. It is a violation of the Eighth Commandment. God is pleading with you. Admit it to Him. You will feel so much better. You will be relieved."

A long, agonizing pause.

Finally, Mr. Purhodi sighed and said, "Let's pray." He pleaded with the Lord to give me courage, convince me of my crime, and forgive me. Then he asked me to pray.

I cried and said nothing.

At the end of this trial, the dean rose to his feet and crunched away on the gravel, leaving me to myself. The sun had already dipped beyond the horizon. The trees lost their brilliance. Only a few scattered clouds reflected the orange glow of the hidden sun.

I did not go inside the cheerful, noisy classroom building. I went around it, straight to the dormitory. I lay on my pillow and wept bitterly.

Chapter 47

The Last Blow

My first reaction was to pack up my meager belongings and head home. Then I thought about my mother; how happy and proud she was that her last child would get a decent education. I also thought about Aleksey Muravyov's mandate to study hard and that I would become their pastor and a schoolteacher. I did not want to come home a loser, and disappoint everybody, especially Mama.

These thoughts helped change my attitude. I put on a psychological seclusion—a form of survival mode. Yes, I was jealous, and jealousy breeds arrogance, pride, a feeling of superiority, even. At that time, I had not known Jesus as my personal Savior and Friend. I learned that much later. I wanted to prove myself to students and staff, show them that I was superior to my male counterparts in class. I had a future. I had a commission—pastor and teacher. I was going to attain my goals on my own.

I refused to participate in student-initiated fun activities. Instead, I spent all my free time studying. I attacked textbooks as if my life depended on them. Being curious and inquisitive, I was easily distracted by my surroundings. In the classroom, I sat in the front row directly in front of the teacher, and took notes furiously. What alleviated my misery was that Mrs. Boynton, the English teacher, was especially nice to me. Having a propensity toward languages, I learned the English language quickly and with good pronunciation. That encouraged me to do even better.

Some of the staff noticed that though I progressed fast, I was an unhappy loner. They took this for my being homesick, longing for home and for my peasant life. To cheer me up, they decided to do something about it.

One day, I was presented a small cage with live ducklings. Instead of rejoicing over the gift, I felt insulted—how dare they treat me like a peasant child! Besides, what was I going to do with them? What would I feed them? I took the ducklings to a shed, on a corner of our property, and turned them loose. In the middle of that shed was a drainpipe. I paid no attention to it and walked out.

Later when I returned, the ducklings disappeared, but I heard peeping somewhere. The sound came from the drainpipe. I looked inside and saw them huddled together, peeping. I panicked. I ran to the dormitory and shouted, "Help," and ran back to the shed. Some boys followed me. One of my classmates, Kosti, peeked into the drainpipe and found a solution.

He constructed a small platform with strings. With the help of a flashlight and a long stick, he lowered the platform and prodded the critters onto the platform. He patiently pulled them out one by one.

I found solace in studying; playing with ducklings didn't suit me. I told Kosti, "They're yours. I don't want them," and walked away. What Kosti did with them, I had no idea, and didn't care.

One Friday, Elder Beitzakhar sent me his own suit and a shirt. The articles of clothing were a bit too big for me, but they were more presentable than my own precious ones.

A couple of months later, Aleksey Muravyov's mother surprised me by appearing at ITS with a pair of pigeons in a cage. At home, I used to raise pigeons. Apparently, someone informed my family that I was lonely and needed something from home to cheer me up. I was very happy to see Aunt Tatiana. However, the "good" news that she confided to me was the last blow.

She informed me, "Jacob, we are so proud of you. The whole church is proud." What she said next devastated me. "We were told that you were falsely accused of stealing a wallet from one of the students. The wallet was found, and the boy came to you and begged your pardon on his knees."

I was stunned. I turned breathless. I tried to compose myself. I stomped my foot and hissed, "Nothing of the sort happened. No one told me that the wallet was found. No one asked me for forgiveness."

Poor Aunt Tatyana tried to quell my ire. She told me some news from home, but none of it registered in my mind. To say I was angry was an understatement. I was mad! That was the meanest thing anyone could do to a sixteen-year-old boy. For the rest of the year, I walked like a pardoned convict, and no one had informed me that I was acquitted.

In a way, I was relieved that I was justified; however, I carried a bitter resentment toward Mr. Purhodi for a long time. Even when he immigrated to the USA and became a docent in the National Museum, Middle-Eastern department, Washington, DC, I never tried to connect with him. I didn't wish him ill, but I didn't want to appear friendly when I disliked him.

During the remaining school year, I isolated myself from the rest of the students and buried myself even deeper in my studies.

I could not find an elevated place for the caged pigeons, so I placed them on top of a wall that was just above my head. I kept them caged for about three weeks and then let them loose, hoping they would return to their roost at night, but they disappeared for good. After a while, I demolished the cage and tossed the planks on top of a refuse pile. Somehow, I identified myself with those caged fowl. I too wished to get lost.

Toward the end of the school year, the Bible teacher placed more emphasis on baptism, preparing students for the blessed event. I put more effort in this class than in any other subject for the wrong reason. I studied not to be converted, but to prove a point—it was my way of showing pride and vengeance.

Finals were fast approaching. The staff and the students plunged into preparation for the culmination of the first year of the religious school in an Islamic country. The classrooms, the dormitories, the grounds, and even the personal grooming were attended to with the utmost care.

The final weekend arrived. Friday Vespers were something special. Singing was enthusiastic. Sermon—inspiring. At the end of the service, the speaker made an earnest altar call, at the end of which the Bible instructor called the baptismal candidates to come forward. Several students stepped toward the platform. I remained seated. Everybody's stare pierced me. I felt hot flashes. I had an urge to run outside, but I didn't want to create an additional scene. They probably had been used to my "weird behavior."

At the end of the service, Mr. Purhodi sat next to me and asked, "Jacob, why didn't you come forward for the baptismal call?"

"I'm not ready," was all I could say, which was true. I could not participate in such a sacred act with a harbored hatred.

"I don't believe it. If anyone, you are most ready. You were on top of the class."

"I'm just not ready," I repeated with irritation. Telling an older person, especially to one in authority, that he was the reason for my refusal was unthinkable.

"I just don't understand you, Jacob." And he walked away.

The last Sabbath of the successful first school year had arrived. It was an exciting day. Nature too smiled upon the occasion. The late spring adorned everything that grew with brilliant colors. The sky was blue, the sun was bright, the air cool and refreshing—everything enhanced the already festive celebration. Relatives, dignitaries, and guests—all in their best outfit, assembled in the chapel. The atmosphere appeared anticipatory.

Students marched in and took their reserved places in the first rows, as usual. Joy and smiles on every face. Guests, staff, friends, and relatives assembled to celebrate us, the students. There were moments when even I was caught up in the festivities. But the nagging feeling of resistance to pressure for baptism prevented me from complete happiness.

Once again, after a stirring sermon by a guest speaker, the baptismal candidates were asked to rise and face the congregation.

I resisted the call. I was miserable. The scenes of the past offences flashed before me. I felt a painful pressure in my chest. How could I bury my ugly feelings into the watery grave? They were deeply rooted. I could not explain my feeling at that time. There was no one to whom I could unload my burden. I felt alien. The joy was not mine.

I don't remember the rest of the holy worship. At the end of the service, Elder Beitzakhar approached me and, in a paternal manner, asked me, "Yasha (an endearing term for "Jacob"), why are you refusing to be baptized?"

"I'm not ready." That's all I could say.

"But why? I don't understand. It's a happy occasion. The baptism will be held at the church in Tehran. It is already beautifully decorated. Many guests will be there. The choir will sing joyful hymns."

"I'm sorry, Mikhail Semyonovich, I can't explain why. Please don't ask me any more questions." I answered with emotion.

Elder Beitzakhar liked me and had taken a personal interest in me. I could feel his genuine interest in my happiness. I did not want to hurt him or be unthankful. I felt miserable. I cried.

He put his arm around me and said, "Don't worry, Yasha, everything will be alright."

I hasten to add that it was not my intention to discredit the school or the missionary faculty. The teaching staff put much effort into making everyone happy and successful. After all, they were preparing students for eternity.

In fact, unbeknownst to me, some godly people paid for my school tuition and even piano lessons. I had no idea that music lessons were given by a private person, Mrs. Gladys Kubrock, an American missionary. In my ignorant peasant mind, I thought missionaries were not paid for such work, that it was a part of school curriculum.

Chapter 48

Back to Rahmatabad

At the end of the Sabbath, the Beitzakhar sisters returned home with their parents and took me with them. The baptismal ceremony was to take place the following Sabbath. I did not attend the baptismal ceremony. Instead, I packed my possessions, and headed home.

By the time I came home, I had already turned seventeen. My voice had changed, and so had my physical appearance, vocabulary, and speech. I was welcomed with open arms. I arrived a hero. After all, I became a city boy, though I hadn't realized it at the time. Finally, I could relax. I was in familiar surroundings where everyone loved and trusted me. My mother was proud of me. She gave me a crushing hug and kissed me.

My return from the capital stirred up curiosity among my relatives and friends.

First Friday evening, when the men returned home from the fields, all the relatives gathered together to check me out. They bombarded me with numerous questions. I told them of the traffic noise; the electric city lights that stayed on all night; that, due to their brightness, one couldn't even see all the stars. What confused them more was my description of people's daily life that defied logic.

For example, I told them, "If you work outside and you need 'to go,' you go inside the house and do your thing. In American English, when you need to relieve yourself, you say, 'I need to go.' In Russian, you say, '*Я хочу на двор*' (yah kha-CHOO na dvor), which means 'I want [to go] outside,' even if you're already outside."

Some of my relatives had no concept of "modern" plumbing. All they knew was an outhouse. They imagined seeing an outhouse in a corner of a one-room house.

Even more strange, was my nature-defying story about a kerosene-operated refrigerator. I explained it this way: "You pour some kerosene into a reservoir at the bottom of a metal box. Then, in special small trays, you pour some cold water and put the trays on the upper shelves, inside the box; after that, you light a wick just above the kerosene reservoir. In a little while, water turns into ice."

At that time, I myself didn't know how Freon behaves under pressure. How could I convince them of this phenomenon?

None of my relatives didn't dare to contradict my stories, lest they offend their now famous son. However, I could tell they were skeptical of my pronouncements. They lost interest in my fantasies; in fact, they appeared disappointed in me.

Then my brother-in-law, Fred Kashirsky, placed his arm around my shoulder and patronizingly said, "You know what, Yasha, it's okay to say such things to us, your relatives, but, please, don't talk about them to anyone else."

"But I'm telling you the truth," I tried to convince him. "I'm not lying. It happens exactly as I described." I was hurt a bit that they didn't believe my stories.

"We know that. We believe you. Just don't mention these things outside our family." He spoke, as if to say, don't take us for fools. We know better than that. Don't embarrass our family. Fire turns water into ice! Huh.

When church elder Aleksey Muravyov heard of my arrival, he asked me to preach in our village church the following Sabbath, Saturday.

I spent long hours preparing for my first sermon.

Sabbath morning, I went to the front of the church, stepped up on a six-inch dirt platform and stood behind the pulpit. All eyes were upon me. I shivered from mixed emotions: fright, guilt, pride.

I opened the Bible to Isaiah, chapter 61, and started reading, "The Spirit of the Lord God is upon me, because the Lord has anointed Me to preach good tidings to the poor; He has sent Me to heal the brokenhearted, to proclaim liberty to the captives, and the opening of the prison to those who are bound..." (NKJV)

I don't remember how many more verses I read, most of which I didn't understand. However, the following words, "To proclaim liberty to the captives, and the opening of the prison to those who are bound," will never be erased from my memory. I invented my own commentary on this passage.

"If you hurt someone and ask for forgiveness," I spoke, "and that person refuses to forgive, it's as if that person is holding you in prison, and God promised to help that person to forgive you: the phrase 'the opening of the prison to those who are bound,'" I explained. "Now, if someone offends you and asks you to forgive that person, and you refuse to forgive, you are holding him in prison. You should ask God to help you let him out of your prison." I looked at Mama. Next to her sat Aunt Masha Guseva, Mama's friend, crying.

I was stunned. I did not expect such a reaction to my words. I was frightened. My conscience began to torment me. How could I preach forgiveness to someone when I myself could not forgive Mr. Purhodi? I could not resolve my dilemma.

While the church service was coming to an end, I was deliberating with myself. I very much wanted to be baptized, but I faced a conundrum. If I was not ready for baptism in Tehran because I carried a grudge at that time, what made me ready now? A grudge is a grudge. Distance does not alter the situation.

My desire for baptism was powerful, so was my pain. There was no one to whom I could turn for advice. The impatient seventeen-year-old wanted his answer on the spot!

I made my decision. In my mind, I presented my case before God and asked Him for forgiveness, and promised to deal with my pain later. Then I asked God for permission to be baptized.

Before the benediction, I announced that I wanted to be baptized. This announcement brought about a loud "Amen!" Mama's face glowed.

The baptismal date was set for the following Sabbath.

On that memorable Sabbath, after church service, the whole congregation marched on the dusty road some two miles toward the Elburz Mountain Range, where there was a water mill with plenty of water.

After a couple of songs, Aleksey Muravyov Baptized me on that warm Sabbath day—the only candidate. Mama wiped her tears.

Gradually, the novelty of my strangeness wore off, and I became just another member of the family. I resumed my previous chores—guarding the watermelon patch. This time, the patch was across the river, *Rechka.* I spent days and nights on the "tower" in isolation. I felt as if I were under house arrest.

Then I began to think about Iran Training School. The offenses I had experienced at the academy didn't seem so painful. I began to miss life in the capital. The village life seemed drab, dirty, smelly.

It was drudgery. I wanted to go back to Tehran.

Chapter 49

Back to Tehran

Unbeknownst to me, God began to shape my future life. Years later, a friend of mine, George Beitzakhar, Elder Beitzakhar's son, told me that my sudden flight at the end of the school year gave his father great concern. He thought that the school officials released me from school, under pretense that nothing useful would become of me. He approached Mr. Paul Boynton and relayed his feelings. He pleaded with the principal to accept me back to school.

The Boyntons were shocked at such an accusation. They were just as puzzled about my sudden disappearance as was Elder Beitzakhar. Paul Boynton convinced Mikhail Beitzakhar that, on the contrary, they saw great potential in me and wanted me back. However, there was one predicament. The Conference was closing the boarding academy for lack of funds. They were planning to continue the education, but under the day-school system.

Studies would be conducted in the basement of the Conference building.

"What are we going to do with Jacob? Where is he going to live?" Mr. Boynton asked.

"No problem, there," replied Elder Beitzakhar. "He will stay with us." Then he added, "He'll attend school with our younger three children."

"Wouldn't that be an imposition on your family?"

"We're used to it. We'll manage."

The Beitzakhars constantly had someone living in their home. I slept on the floor in Elder Beitzakhar's father's bedroom.

Decision made, Elder Beitzakhar went into action. He asked Elder Daniel Kubrock, Mrs. Kubrock's husband, to go after me and bring me back to Tehran.

Elder Kubrock borrowed the Conference vehicle, the ambulance they had purchased from the U.S. Army, and decided to rescue me from the drudgery of village life.

Elder Beitzakhar took his son, George. The rescue mission took two days to reach Rahmatabad.

They stayed a whole week in our village, using the church building for their lodging until returning home to Tehran.

I, then, lived with the Beitzakhars a short while. They were extremely hospitable. Besides their five children, their home was always full of friends and relatives.

Mrs. Beitzakhar, Anastasia, was a hard-working, industrious woman. To supplement her husband's income, she constantly knitted children's clothing for various clothing stores. Her specialty was knitting and crocheting. In fact, the Beitzakhar home was like a workshop. Anastasia had taught her children her art, and she inducted me into their workshop.

During evenings and holidays, after we did our homework, we all, self included, sat in the family room, knitting and listening to the radio.

My other job was hand-pumping water into the water tank situated on the attic. Every morning, except on Sabbaths, I would descend into the basement and start pumping. As I pumped, I counted in English—mastering the English language. Six days a week, all four of us, Flora, Liza, George, and I traveled to "school" on public transportation. The Beitzakhars didn't own a car.

Chapter 50

Life in an American Family

Shortly after WWII, the young Shah of Iran requested military personnel from the United States government to train his own counterparts. Some of the U.S. Army personnel responded to the invitation and moved to Iran with their families.

The American trainers had interpreters, but their families were left in quandary. Wives needed to get out of the house and do some shopping, but they spoke no Farsi. Interpreters were at a premium.

Here, Mrs. Ruth Boynton came to the rescue of a sergeant's wife, Mrs. Marilyn Curl—and me. She found me a job with the Curl family in the capacity of a houseboy, a cook, an interpreter and a nanny to their three children. I fulfilled all the house chores the women normally did. But from the start, I requested to be relieved from doing the laundry. I agreed to do women's work. Washing someone's underwear was beneath me—I wanted to reserve some personal dignity.

Mrs. Curl honored my request, and never subjected me to do the mean job. However, I did hang the clothes on the line and iron them. The sheets, pillowcases, and Sergeant Curl's military uniform I took to the cleaners.

Mrs. Curl instructed me to list every item taken to the cleaners. At first, I had a problem with naming and spelling laundry items. I did list them on a piece of paper, but alas, my spelling left something to be desired. One day, Mrs. Curl looked at the list and congratulated me on my accomplishment. However, she pointed out that my spelling of the word "sheets" was incorrect. She corrected my spelling, adding that my spelling of the word had another meaning in English. She told me its meaning.

I was embarrassed. Strange as it seems, I also felt somewhat proud. I had learned my first bad word in English. A word that one doesn't learn at a desk in a classroom. I did not share my discovery with anyone. After all, I was studying to be a preacher.

Overseeing three innocent children aged two to six increased my vocabulary of human anatomy and bathroom language—my spelling too. Such knowledge one learns either living in a family or attending a university.

I learned many other things. Occasionally, the Curls hosted guests, other American military families. On those occasions, Sgt. Curl taught me how to mix and name different types of liquor. Once, out of curiosity, I tasted a Bloody Mary— just a teaspoon. I didn't like it. That was the end of my alcoholism.

Initially, when I started working for the Curls, I was treated like a servant. I ate my meals in the kitchen, not at the table with the family. I expected that. However, when I spent more quality time with the children than did their parents, the little ones became attached to me and insisted that I eat meals with the family, as if I were their older brother. Soon, I was invited to share meals at the family table.

Mrs. Curl saw to it that my table manners were observed according to the times of that era. That is another lesson I learned that was not taught in a classroom. In no time, I felt comfortable at the table, as if I was part of the family.

I experienced something else too. Some Iranian officers' wives would invite American wives to their house, to taste Persian cuisine and to expand each other's knowledge of their cultures. Hosting foreigners, especially the Americans at that time, added some prestige. Usually, neither the Iranian nor the American counterpart knew each other's language. In absence of interpreters, they requested my services—an eighteen-year-old teenager.

I felt quite awkward to be inside a rich Iranian home, translating woman talk. It embarrassed me. As far as these Iranian wealthy women were concerned, I was merely a servant, and my personal life was none of their concern; in fact, I was a nonentity. I despised my assignment, but considering the alternative, translating women's gossip trumped flinging animal dung in a barn.

Mrs. Marilyn Curl and her children, who were my charge.

Jacob at 19: Servant, nanny, and teacher.

Chapter 51

Teaching Experience

Mrs. Boynton always looked after me and always came to my aid. One day, she asked me to teach English to some students from the University of Tehran. I almost had a cardiac arrest—me teaching English to university students? No way!

"I cannot do that," I remonstrated. "I'm just beginning to study the English language myself. How can I teach it to university students?"

"You can," she insisted with a smile. "I can help you. These students are only beginning. I'm sure you can do it. Besides, you will be paid for it. How about it?"

"I don't know. I have to think about it." I responded weakly. Extra money was the bait.

"They want *us* to teach them." Mrs. Boynton explained. "We don't have time to do that. So, I thought about you. It's a great opportunity. Some money in a pocket is a good feeling. I need the answer now. I must let them know tomorrow—to accept them or turn them down. I'll handle all the arrangements myself. All you need to do is teach twice a week. They will pay the Conference, and I'll pay you. Agreed?"

After a long confusing silence, I mumbled with a whisper, "I guess so," and then added, "How about Sgt. Curl? Will he give me time off?"

"I'll take care of that. Don't worry about it." Mrs. Boynton was a superb persuader.

I felt stunned. Before I knew what was happening, I was hired. Mrs. Boynton provided elementary textbooks and gave me a copy of each. Then she gave me some points on instruction and on art of teaching. I was very nervous. I went over the textbooks repeatedly, rehearsing as an actor getting ready for stage.

Instead of assigning us to one of the rooms in the basement, the school staff offered us a Conference room with a large table and several soft chairs.

The dreadful day arrived.

With trepidation, I opened the door to the "classroom."

Just as I stepped in, students rose to their feet and stood at attention. I froze and almost fell off my feet. I took hold of myself and said, "Be seated."

After they complied, I introduced myself. I told them to call me "Jacob." I did not want to be addressed by any other title. Then I asked for their names. There were four boys and two girls—all my age. They were all dressed formally.

I spoke to them in perfect Farsi. They were confounded. How was it possible that this non-Persian-looking person spoke their language so fluently? They treated me as if I were some professor. These students were no ordinary people. They were very bright. I was surprised at how quickly they grasped the English language.

Because I enjoyed studying with those pleasant young people, I decided to make teaching my profession. A teacher I did become, but a pastor, not.

Mrs. Boynton charmed Sgt. Curl, and he agreed to let me stay a couple of hours longer away from home twice a week. Later, he enrolled his two older children into the elementary school at the Mission with the missionaries' children.

I experienced another privilege: An American Sergeant dressed in US military uniform drove his children and me in a Jeep to school. No more public transportation for me. I felt important.

A few weeks later, Mrs. Boynton brought me another student, the daughter of a Saudi Arabian

Ambassador. She was about the same age as the rest of the students. I gave this teenager private lessons.

Mrs. Boynton paid me 1,600 rials a month. In today's money, it would be about $100. For my first month's salary, I purchased a waterproof watch. I felt I was climbing up the social ladder.

What I didn't know was that the university students took me for an American—a son of one of the missionaries. It wasn't until December of 1950, when I was getting ready to immigrate to America that they discovered who I really was.

They were shocked when they found out I was not an American. I wondered if they demanded a refund, when they realized that they had been taught by an "impostor."

Chapter 52

Lesson on Humility

Though I enjoyed the respect from my students, I encountered a bitter lesson on humility. One day, Mrs. Curl was invited for a visit by the wife of an Iranian military officer. Marilyn dressed herself and her children properly. I followed suit.

An expensive looking car drove up to the Curl's rented house. We boarded. I had never touched such a luxurious automobile before, let alone ride in one. The chauffer drove us up to a closed rod-iron gate and honked. A servant ran up to the gate and opened it with difficulty. The car rolled over a curved driveway and stopped at the front door of a sumptuous building. The chauffer opened the doors for us, as if for some dignitaries, and we exited awkwardly.

Here was a reversal of social roles. The women of the American military personnel received some lessons at home on Iranian culture and etiquette, but they had not expected to be hosted by high-class Iranian families. In America, a sergeant's wife was considered a middle-class person.

Conversely, in Iran at that time, an American woman, especially, was looked upon as something exotic, something from half way around the world.

And bringing along a "handsome" male teenage nanny, instead of an old woman, was something uncommon, too. For the high-class women, to host such an "extraterrestrial" friendly person added a distinct prestige.

So, Marilyn Curl was a special guest. I'm sure she behaved properly. After all, she was an alien, and aliens were above criticism. Besides, she was the wife of Sergeant Curl who worked with an Iranian officer on equal ground, and who trained Iranian military personnel. He was treated with high respect.

As a teacher to the students of the elite, I was shown the same respect as Sgt. Curl. However, I was only a high school student and a country boy, giving lessons to university students from prestigious families.

On this occasion, though, the officer's wife invited an interpreter, a good-looking young woman, probably a university student. I was relieved from the embarrassing duty.

However, my relief turned into humiliation. The officer's wife asked me to stay outside and mind the children in the company of the many house servants. These serfs could not figure me out—an American-looking young man thrust into an illiterate bunch of servants.

The front yard had a swimming pool, a tennis court, decorative well-trimmed trees, and roses galore. An eight-foot brick wall enclosed the expansive estate. Being a servant, I was prohibited from swimming in the pool or play tennis. Servants were forbidden to play with the masters' play-things.

It was quite normal for an Iranian woman with some status in society to send her guest's servants to join the company of her own counterparts. A servant is a servant, and he or she belonged with the other servants. They all had something in common. No servant was ever treated on the same level with a master. This woman didn't know that I was not a "servant" in the normal sense of the word.

I was hurt. After all, in the classroom, I was treated by the rich university students as a professor, and by my employer as a member of the family.

Here I was relegated to the lowest class of people as riffraff. It was a bitter, but an important lesson in humility for me.

Part XI

Chapter 53

Immigration

The time came for me to emigrate to America. The promise that Aleksey Muravyov made to me, building a new church and a school for me, were no longer binding. Like many other Russian families, the Muravyovs abandoned Rahmatabad and had immigrated to America.

Most of us who had lived in Iran were of stateless status. When we escaped from the Soviet Union nineteen years earlier, the Persians accepted us graciously. Remember, one landowner even evicted villagers from their own village to accommodate us. On top of that, he offered us all the land we could till. People were hospitable and generous.

When it came to business and civil laws, things were different. In business dealings, there was one rule—bribery. As Russians say, *Ne podmazhesh, ne poyedesh,* "You won't grease, you won't go." At that time, the Iranian government issued us, the stateless people, special passports, forms of pass or permission of passage.

A person traveling to any city had to have written, stamped permission, indicating destination and duration of stay in that city. When that person arrived at his destination, he was obliged to report to city authorities and present the documents, informing them of his arrival. The same routine was required on the return trip.

On the other hand, citizens of Iran could freely travel inside the country. Some Russians from our village decided to apply for Iranian citizenship. Citizenship relieved them of certain troubles in dealing with capricious officials.

However, this privilege turned out to be a high liability. When the United States began to accept stateless people into their country, the wait time for stateless Russians was two years, and if they obtained American farmers as sponsors, there was no wait time.

For citizens of Iran, the wait time was twenty years. Those who adopted Iranian citizenship found themselves in a bind. When they tried to reverse their political preference, they faced herculean hardships. In the end, they did surmount their labors, but it cost them a fortune.

Like my father, I hated bribes.

It was December of 1950. I needed to arrange the preliminaries for immigration to America. I had to run a long list of errands such as securing a visa application from the U. S. Embassy, getting medical exams, obtaining a series of immunizations.

There was no problem dealing with American personnel, but when it came time to deal with some of the Iranian officials, I had to do a lot of hateful "greasing."

The Curls had been very gracious to me in permitting me time to run around Tehran obtaining all these documents.

The final phase of these activities was the most difficult. I resigned from teaching and asked for time off from the Curls. Now, I had to travel to Rahmatabad, bring my mother to Tehran, and then get all her documents in order.

By this time, I had mastered some Iranian tricks on bribery. I headed to Tehran police headquarters. A document from Tehran police authorities carried with it heavy weight. I requested their permission to travel to Rahmatabad to bring my mother to Tehran. This was to be written on my "passport," signed and stamped.

I did not mind "greasing" at this point.

With potent ammunition in hand, I foretasted battle with weaker authorities. No more "greasing" I anticipated! Surprise!

Early, the following morning, I tied my bare necessities in a bundle and boarded a third-class car without seats on a train. The car was full of noisy peasant people with their fowl and animals. You can imagine the noise, smell, and ruckus. But my main aim was to bring my mother to Tehran—we were going to America.

The end of the railroad line stopped at Bandar Shah, a port city on the Caspian Sea. I arrived there late afternoon. From there I boarded a bus to Gorgon and stayed overnight in a Russian-operated inn.

The following morning, after a hasty breakfast at the inn, I went to the "bus" station and sat in the front seat behind the driver of a half-full Volkswagen bus.

The trip started comfortably, at first. And then at every village stop along the Shah's Highway, more passengers, mostly women, boarded with their foul chickens, lambs and goats. Soon the bus was so packed with passengers that the driver's assistant had to use his knee to force travelers into the vehicle and shut the door behind them. He, himself, had to stand outside on a step, clinging onto the door handles for his dear life.

On the way to Rahmatabad in a VW (Volkswagen) bus on the Shah's Highway in 1977.

The end of the line for me was Fazelabad. I extricated myself from the packed, smelly VW bus. I slung my possessions over my shoulder, and walked the three-mile trek to our home in Rahmatabad. As soon as I arrived home, I told Mama to pack immediately. We were going to America.

"But, son," she remonstrated, "we have to have a farewell dinner for the church and relatives."

"We can't wait for dinner," I insisted firmly. "We have no time! Besides, I have a job, there."

Mama was shocked. As if, she thought, *My baby is ordering me what to do?*

That evening, we informed our close relatives and church members of our departure. There were only a handful of them that came over. Many villagers were already in America, and some were in Tehran waiting for their departure papers.

All our relatives were upset with me for not allowing my mother to make a proper farewell departure. After all, Mama was a respected member not only in our church, but also in the whole community. I was adamant. I did not want to be absent a long time from my job.

The family put together a scanty evening dinner. It was a grand occasion for tears. This was not an ordinary goodbye; it was a genuine farewell. Other villagers came by for the tear-shedding occasion. All expressed their disapproval of my behavior. I could read their minds, "Is that what you learned at the capital city—to be rude and disrespectful to generations of established culture?" They peered at me as if I was an enemy.

Early next morning, Aleksey hitched his horses to a wagon and took us to Fazelabad. Mama and I caught a truck to Gorgon. The driver dropped us off in the center of the city. There, we caught a droshky, a horse-drawn taxi, and went directly to the police station to obtain a pass for Mama. We'd been there many times before.

We went up to the second floor, heading toward the official's department in charge of issuing passes and other permits. The door to his office was wide open, his desk facing the doorway. We approached the door and I asked, "May we come in?"

Last photo of mama and me before trekking to America.

The tall, middle-aged skinny man said sweetly, "*Behfarmoeed*" (Please, enter). We entered, and I greeted him with a smirk. "*Salaam alaikum.*"

He responded sweetly, "*Alaikum salaam,*" and added, just as sweetly but in businesslike fashion, "*Khohesh mikunam, besheeneed*" (Please, be seated).

He anticipated a grand gratuity. We had already met each other on previous occasions when I needed to travel to other cities.

I took my passport out and opened it to the page where capital city authorities had written a directive, to all concerned, giving me permission to bring my mother to Tehran. Along with my mother's passport, I ceremonially handed both documents to this official.

He perused mine. Immediately, his pleasantness evaporated. He read it again, turned it every which way. Finally, he grunted, wrote something in Mama's passport, and signed it.

He was about to stamp the document and give both back to me, when he suddenly froze. Then he placed both passports on his desk, leaned back in his soft chair, placed his hands behind his head, and said, "The people in Tehran wrote that you should bring your mother to Tehran, but they did not specify that I should permit your mother to travel with you. What are you going to do about it?"

I was about to protest, but he rose from his chair and said, "I'll step into my office for a while. You and your mother decide what to do about this issue." Then he turned around and slicked into his lair.

I knew exactly what he had in mind. He was giving us time to decide on the amount of the bribe.

But he overlooked one thing: he left the passports on his desk. I thought to myself, *You're not going to get away with this.* I gave Mama a sign of silence, then filched the documents off the desk, grabbed our possessions, and tiptoed out of the trap trembling.

We flew out of that place as fast as Mama's legs could carry her, caught a droshky, and sped directly to the bus station.

We arrived at Bandar Shah late in the day. Rather than stop at this city and catch the train in the morning, we wanted to be as far from Gorgon as possible. I was afraid the Gorgon police tentacles would catch up with us.

We stopped at some of Mama's friends for the night. In the morning, without having breakfast, we caught a train to Tehran. It was not until the train moved on its tracks that I felt safe. To me, all this stress was worth not paying the bribe. I stuck to my principles.

As soon as we arrived in Tehran, I deposited Mama at my sister Anna's place, and set in motion a new phase of arranging for our departure to America.

At that time, the Iranian mint had just issued the smallest denomination of paper currency, five rials, about 25 cents in US currency. I sped to the bank and supplied myself with a handful of such paper money. Then, I purchased some envelopes and inserted one bill into each envelope. Having supplied myself with the right amount of "ammunition," I launched a blitzkrieg against enemy forces.

With the list of agencies and certain clearances we needed, such as the ubiquitous police, exit visas, obtaining mug shots, I waged my war against bribery. Not once did an agent turn down the obligatory bribe.

Here was my strategy. As soon as an official welcomed me, offered me a seat, and asked me what I wanted, I voiced my request, meanwhile, noticeably slipping an envelope with a five-tumon note under his desk-sized blotting paper.

Five-tumon currency, front side.

Five-tumon currency, back side.

I could've slipped an empty envelope, but I still had respect for government employees—or was it fear of being caught? I preferred being considered a "cheapskate" to being insolent.

Now, when I look back some sixty-nine years later, I do regret not being honorable.

With proper documentation in our possession, I successfully dragged my mother through the labyrinth of the Iranian government and U.S. embassy. We were ready for immigration.

⁂   ⁂   ⁂

It was Wednesday morning, December 28, 1950, when the Boyntons, the Kubrocks, and some members of the Beitzakhar family drove my mother and me to Mehrabad International Airport.

We boarded a British Overseas Airways Corporation (BOAC) "prop" plane and bade farewell to Iran which, before 1935, was known throughout the world as "Persia." With a roar of the engines, we soared into the air, and abandoned Iran, never to return to this country. That is what the exit visa stated.

Our final trek to the United States of America, on a British Overseas Airways Corporation (BOAC) prop plane.

Epilogue

*Ask the former generations and find out what
their fathers learned, for we were born only
yesterday and know nothing, and our days on
earth are but a shadow.*
Job 8: 8-9, NIV

My dear descendants, you have begged me to
write the history of our Volkov past. With
God's help, I have responded to your request to the
best of my knowledge, research, and ability.

Some of you might be disappointed with me
because I did not write more about your relatives.
Every single person in this book could provide an
abundance of exciting and unique information. Had
I attempted to please all of you, it would have filled
many volumes. Unfortunately, I don't have that
many years left in me. So, please accept this book as
is. I warned in the beginning not to complain.

I am, nonetheless, leaving something special
for each of you. All of you are educated enough

to read this book. Most of your ancestors did not have the privilege you possess; but with limited school education and faith, they had more precious "stuff"—and it is my wish that you will claim this for yourselves—their unwavering trust in God.

Our escape from Soviet Russia, in 1931, resembled the flight of the Israelites from Egypt. In both instances, refugees escaped in anxious speed. Both were pursued by military forces, carrying with them necessary provisions and possessions, as well as their own "baggage."

Now, it took the Israelites forty years of wandering through the wilderness before they reached Canaan. They all, twenty years and older, perished with their "baggage," except two of them, Joshua and Caleb.

In the case of your ancestors, something similar transpired. It took them approximately the same number of years to trek from Central Russia to America. Most of your predecessors never made it to their earthly Canaan, America. Their bodies, like those of the Israelites, are scattered throughout the "wilderness"—Russia, the Caucasus, Turkmenistan and Iran.

There is a big difference, though, between the Israelites and your "foretrekkers." The former were compelled to wander through the wilderness for *disobeying* God; the latter, for *obeying* Him.

The Israelite survivors did reach their Canaan, but when life became comfortable for them, they forgot God's guidance. Consequently, they lost their inheritance.

You, the survivors of your forerunners, have your "Canaan," America, the land of freedom. Don't get so comfortable that you forget who you are, and how God led your forefathers, and, in the end, lose your "inheritance." Make God your priority.

Don't forget, there are more choices to be made on your trek to your Eternal Home. On this journey, your choice will not rest on what to take with you, nor what to abandon, but with how tightly you are tied down to your earthly possessions. We are told we can take with us nothing. Absolutely NOTHING!

Not even our "baggage."

Make the right choices!

And one more thing. When a willful child disregards his or her parents' wise guidance, the parents might apply Solomon's rod to point the child in the right direction. When trials and pains come your way—and come they will—don't blame

God. Consider it a kick to your posterior to direct you onto the right path.

For, when you follow the right path, you can expect great rewards. After all, you are trekking to the Heavenly Canaan.